About the C

Artwork for the cover was created by Roy Young illustrating Tonia Madenford's contribution to Kim Carlsberg's book *The Art of Close Encounters*, published in 2010 by Close Encounters Publishing.

The story, *Playing Amongst the Stars*, recounts Madenford's contact experiences as a child. Both Roy Young and Tonia Madenford have had childhood contact experiences and resonate with the thesis of Neil Gould's work.

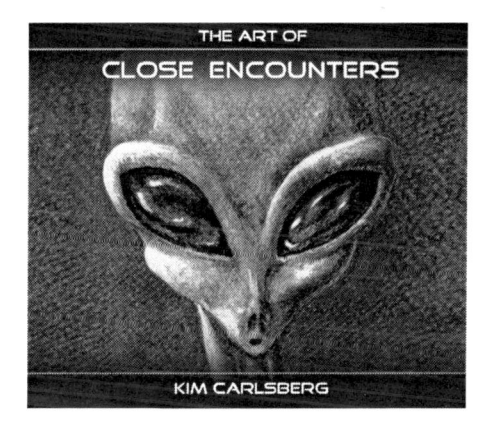

"My artwork is inspired by personal experiences and I consider ADHD a divine gift that has been long misunderstood."~ *Roy Young*

"Those with this gift tend to be full of energy, move quickly between spaces, communicate in pictures, and think largely 'outside the box'. What wonderful attributes and star-based traits! Perhaps what we are really observing is human evolution and significant changes within consciousness and DNA."~ *Tonia Madenford*

Cover Design: Larry Lowe
Art: ©2007 Roy Young
Publication: The Art of Close Encounters
ISBN 978-1-4507-3268-0
Close Encounters Publishing
TheArtOfCloseEncounters.com
CloseEncountersPublishing.com

In memory of:

Pearl Salmo who always treated me with respect

Close Encounters
of the
ADHD Kind

*To Chris
Enjoy!
Andrea (Gould) Birbeck*

Neil Gould

authorHOUSE®

AuthorHouse™ UK Ltd.
500 Avebury Boulevard
Central Milton Keynes, MK9 2BE
www.authorhouse.co.uk
Phone: 08001974150

© 2010 Neil Gould. All rights reserved.

No part of this book may be reproduced, stored in a retrieval system, or transmitted by any means without the written permission of the author.

First published by AuthorHouse   10/4/2010

ISBN: 978-1-4520-3785-1 (sc)

The layout of the chapter headings were inspired by the book 'The Catchers of Heaven' written by the late Dr Michael Wolf

This book is printed on acid-free paper.

This book is a work of non-fiction. Names and places have been changed to protect the privacy of all individuals. The events and situations are true.

The reader should consult with their physician in matters relating to any symptoms that may require medical attention; this book is not a substitute for advice from the medical profession.

My special thanks to:

Louise, for your unrelenting belief in me.

My kids Jake Liat Zak, my wife Jackie;
my Mother and family for putting up with me.

The Exopolitics Institute, Hawaii. A place of learning;
founded by Dr Michael Salla PhD and assisted by
Angelike Whitecliff.
&
To Paula Harris M.Ed, Manuel Lamiroy Lic. Juris,
Rebecca Hardcastle PhD,
Dr Michael Salla PhD and Angelika Whitecliff
for the Certifications Programs that they
teach to the world within the Exopolitics Institute.

Spider webs form complex circular patterns; their strands radiate outwards. I never solved the riddle of how the spider sent its web from one side of the stream to the other. It was not the wind, I assure you. Every strand of web in a different direction, but in the end the story is the same. Through quantum entanglement all strands lead to the one web.

My thanks to:
Nicola Shannon for the Editing of this book.
Alan Brody and Philip Chu (Cheuk Fei) for the illustrations.

My appreciation to:
Roy Young for designing the graphics on this cover.
Larry Lowe for the creation of this book cover.
Tonia Madenford and Kim Carlsberg for graciously sharing their graphics.

Most of all to:
> **My Star Visitors, for the journey**

Contents

Endorsements xi
INTRODUCTION 1
Chapter 1 3
    Borne Into Chaos

Chapter 2 8
    The New Neighborhood

Chapter 3 12
    A Real Out-Of This-World Experience Or Society Would Tell Me I Imagined It

Chapter 4 18
    Breaking the Rules Or Do As I Say, Not As I Do

Chapter 5 22
    A Black Angel saves our White Skins

Chapter 6 26
    The Third World War

Chapter 7 30
    Us vs. Them Or Antics and impulse

Chapter 8 34
    Missing time Or Close Encounter of the ADD kind

Chapter 9 42
    The crumbling of the self-esteem Or You cannot feel what I can see from here

Chapter 10 47
    Toy Soldiers Or Mind Control

Chapter 11 53
    Like attracts like Or Funny people like Jack and me

Chapter 12 62
    Dumped naked Or Make your own way home

Chapter 13 66
    Kaapi – Garland & I loved him more than ourselves Or A mystical mystic, bathed in alcohol and dagga

Chapter 14 73
    Check my 'tumb, I live in hell but I love you Or Come to the white man's world, it's safe at Smuggler's Inn

Chapter 15.. 81
    Enter: The Hypnotist Or The Ventriloquist Who Was an Articled Clerk

Chapter 16.. 87
    Africa Adieu– I miss you, you are in my bones Or Pendennis Castle to the UK Or What the hell am I doing here, in this dump?

Chapter 17.. 96
    My jobs or The Egyptian With A Hole In His Shirt or Climbing the corporate ladder - Jew Boy

Chapter 18.. 111
    First sale of business Or Do not use the Loo

Chapter 19 118
    Enter: my wife Jackie Or She was chosen for me

Chapter 20. 122
    Andrea The first ADD UK charity Or Born again, the fog clears

Chapter 21. 131
    Enter: My first Child

Chapter 22. 133
    Depression in the UK Or Why don't you go back to South Africa? Or I Hate Your Brussels Sprouts

Chapter 23. 142
    The break - in and robbery Or You can steal but you cannot kill me – I know your mind

Chapter 24. 146
    Return of the radiant light beings Or Out of body experience

Chapter 25. 154
    Leaving the UK Or The UK has a divine purpose in giving people a sense of proportion

Chapter 26. 160
    My new life in People's Republic of China Or You will not believe the people over here

Chapter 27. 176
    What is so clever about an electronic unit?

Chapter 28. 182
    Men in black – with long beards Or Impossible task

Chapter 29. 205
    Why can't you be like them? or Wolves in sheep's clothing

Chapter 30.. 208
 Defragmentation

Chapter 31.. 216
 Never call anyone stupid again Or The caller of names do not know their own name

Chapter 32.. 222
 The World Is 1000 Times Faster Than 40 Years Ago Or Evolution - a Reason For ADHD or Enter: Dr Greer and Exit: Dr Mack

Chapter 33.. 230
 Death of a parent Or ADHD celebration of life

Chapter 34.. 237
 How does ET Disclosure make any difference to your life? Or Leave me in my comfort zone please

Chapter 35.. 245
 Why don't the Star Visitors show themselves?

Chapter 36.. 256
 The Finale

Bibliography 259
About the Author 261

Endorsements

Close Encounters of the ADHD Kind; an ongoing experience with extra-terrestrials. An ADHD challenged author wired into a multidimensional reality, an ET gift. As Principal of ACERN (Australian Close Encounter resource network) I feel such a book is long overdue. A number of researchers myself included, find it curious that ADHD is becoming increasingly commonplace and that many with ADHD have ET related experiences, and we have to ask the reason why?

Although ADHD is conventionally accepted as a human dysfunction, these individuals are normally highly intelligent, although the ADHD individual is easily distracted with learning difficulties, and has little fear of consequences. ADHD is viewed as a handicap in our human socialization, and education programs. But it may well be these very qualities that will help to advance humanity from its limited third dimensional mindset, as Neil suggests in his book. He believes his ADHD offers him a unique gift, the ability to separate himself from conventional, limiting educational and social expectations, to see outside of the third dimensional box, and helps them to avoid being controlled by limited human programs and beliefs.

In his story Neil is brutally honest about his life which is refreshing in itself. His honesty is translated into his own multidimensional story, and contact with ET intelligences. His intuitive abilities and OBE's (Out of body experiences) with 'liquid light' the experience of dimensional hyperspace, and 'cosmic downloads'; which he terms an exo-conscious reality. Neil has opened up Pandora's Box by suggesting that ADHD maybe new software for Homo sapiens to give them abilities to perceive a broader multi dimensional reality. It is a hypotheses that has merit given my research into the Star Children, and the fact that my latest research shows many complex programs and DNA manipulation that could well explain that ADHD is not so much a dysfunction, but one of the new programs for upgrading our species. If this is so we are in for an interesting ride as an evolving species.

Mary Rodwell RN, ACERN

Australian Close Encounter Resource Network

http://www.acern.com.au/

Neil Gould's *Close Encounters of the ADHD Kind: An Ongoing Experience with Extraterrestrials,* is a significant and beguiling autobiography of ongoing extraterrestrial contact and its effect on beliefs and behavior. Coming to grips with ADHD, amplified by a panoply of paranormal events and extraterrestrial communications, Gould transforms the cognitive dissonance and cultural intolerance of ADHD into advanced consciousness, Exoconsciousness.

A study in the extraterrestrial dimensions and abilities of personal consciousness, his book provides a phenomenological description of the angst and thrill of experiencing advanced consciousness. One of Gould's familiar homes is Extraterrestrial Reality.

The reader follows Gould's hyperactive childhood trajectory, as he charges head-long, breaking every rule and battling for positions outside the box of normalized belief systems. It is a story of courage and creativity as well as trauma. Time and again he is abused, abandoned, and attacked. His boyhood terrain of South Africa is simultaneously mystical and brutal. As a result his brain, like a metronome, clicks between seeking creative stimulation amid a brain riddled with paralyzing trauma scars. Leap—scar—leap—scar. Trauma becomes a perfect recipe for his relentless cognitive obsession with risk, that is more often than not, rewarded with punishment, isolation, and a brick wall of cultural tradition. His ADHD cry echoing, "What's wrong with everyone?"

Gaining Exoconsciousness, as a Planet Earth enterprise, by necessity, confronts one with the grim residue of trauma. This is true for most, if not, all extraterrestrial contactees. Trauma is a primary filter for contact experience. As a result, humans learn to flinch and fight when striving to integrate strange experiences, especially paranormal. As Gould testifies, ADHD "high alert" development is the primary framework for functioning in the 3D world. Traumatologist, Robert Scaer, asserts that all human psychopathology and disease is rooted in trauma scarring. Clear or rewire trauma scars to find health and happiness.

Gould rewires by taking another leap. He prevails by reaching beyond his brain into the multiverse of consciousness. He likens it to a computer browser where new screens appear to relieve human imposed boundaries. A lifespan of extraterrestrial contact, including downloads, communications, and experiences, launches him, at an early age, into Exoconcious dimensions. The answer to his ADHD cry of "What's wrong with everyone" is "They don't live where I do."

For Gould, the multiverse of consciousness is the Holy Grail of brain balance. Here his body bound brain is trumped by consciousness, roaming fields of extraterrestrial life. In these fields, Earth events are translated and reprioritized. The result is a lessening of importance of Earth 3D life. The reader feels Gould relax and lean into his paranormal experience. Safe haven.

His brain, that could be viewed as a conflicting belief system of trauma vs. paranormal, instead exhibits a kind of yin and yang brain balance. Preeminent contactee researcher, John Mack referenced the impact of the trauma reaction filter of ET contact. He noted its prevalence, and then gently guided his patients past its panic portals into spiritual perspective. Mack called the process, "fencing the fear". He fenced fear with talk therapy. Gould fenced his fear with courage. Again and again he entered the world of the paranormal and overcame it's culturally imposed sideshow horrors. He saw the paranormal horror as illusion and thereby flourished.

Reading Gould's autobiography, it becomes quickly apparent that our culture is populated with numerous ADHD diagnosed persons who, if given the opportunity to speak freely, would confess to often living in an alternative reality. Some of them dwell in an Exoconscious Reality. Gather this Exoconscious clan and there is a significant planetary population ready to embrace a world beyond trauma of flinching and fighting. This world beyond is rapidly being populated and created by Exopolitics and Exoconscious educators and activists who acknowledge Gould's alternative reality as historically and scientifically valid. Nomadic ADHD nonconformists like Gould can now settle down and form roots, supported by a verifiable foundation that accepts paranormal as normal. It is the future home of many.

Dr Rebecca Hardcastle PhD

http://www.exoconsciousness.com/

While ADHD is conventionally viewed as a special learning disorder for those trying to progress through a 'normal' education system, ADHD better designates a non-conventional way of learning that promises to incorporate a greater assortment of perspectives and ideas. The behavior of those with ADHD is analogous to one trying to break out from the small confines of the human brain socialized to think in linear terms in understanding the world, into a non-physical expression of consciousness that operates in distinctly non-linear ways in grasping the hidden mysteries of life. It is this non-conventional model of learning and behavior that one encounters in Neil Gould's book, Close Encounters of the ADHD Kind. It is this ability to think outside the box that leads Mr. Gould to tackle some of the most challenging issues that defy conventional learning modalities. Arguably none are as challenging as the presence of extraterrestrial life which confronts one intellectually, emotionally, physically and spiritually. He introduces the reader to this presence through a series of synchronistic personal experiences, together with the insights of a select group of researchers into the extraterrestrial phenomenon. This is a book that will open many doors to a phenomenon that is destined to profoundly change life on this planet; and will deeply alter the way we go about educating ourselves about one another, the universe and life itself.

Michael E. Salla, Ph.D.

Founder, Exopolitics Institute

Neil Gould is a man of many fascinating parts. His book brilliantly reflects these and does more than justice to his life experience. It is an essential read and comprises outlooks, ideas and insights whose time has come. There are doubtless many in the world who have experienced his challenges but failed to comprehend the precise nature of their difficulties. This book will open their eyes, put their minds at rest, while helping to galvanise them into realizing their full potential. There are certainly even larger numbers of people who have interacted with such individuals and utterly failed to understand them or been bemused, possibly angered and very definitely irritated by their conduct. This book will explain so much to them as to enrich, nurture and enliven their future relationships in the most positive and constructive way.

"Close Encounters of the ADHD Kind" comprises in part a truly riveting autobiography written with disarming candour, but it is also a deeply penetrating commentary on the human condition in what is generally regarded as a state of existence involved with managing the challenges dealt out by our understanding of conventional life, either enhanced or exacerbated by those who contend with the ADD/ADHD malady.

However, it is so much more than this. For the denouement towards the end of his writing is to be found in his profound insight and extraordinary understanding of the broader esoteric human experience, our reasons for choosing to come here, for the painful exposure to indeed being here and leading largely distressing though educational lives in a multi-dimensional paradigm massively enriched (if we will only allow it to be) by the expansion of our consciousness into staggering new realms wherein our real potential is realized and all aspirations are possible. Equally importantly, and finally, it will give the reader the confidence to face death, the final and unavoidable supreme adventure each and every human being reluctantly contemplates, with tranquility, resolve and understanding.

This amazing story is the saga of one man's struggle to come to terms with the fact that he was different in an age when that difference was neither understood nor identified, born and bred into an agonized South African society, itself suffering from artificially contrived social, economic and political constraints and consequently very real social and political stresses and strains. It is the record of his gradual realization that he was indeed functioning on a different mental and spiritual plane and at a different psychological level to that of his family, friends and acquaintances. It is a reflection of his courage and tenacity in seeking to constantly improve himself, his understanding of himself and hence his ability to relate to and assist his fellow man and woman, and in so doing to carve out a brilliant career, initially in England but later in the Far East, surviving in the most cut throat of industries in the most intensely ruthless of entrepreneurial environments with brutal operators and unscrupulous actors. In learning to cope with his ADHD condition, he discovered that his abilities to read and relate to people of diverse backgrounds, origins and aspirations were vastly enhanced way above the norm to an astonishing intuitive and psychic degree. Moreover, these qualities enabled him to understand circumstances and situations both on a personal basis and an international level with a discernment and acuity so profound and far reaching that it leaves the reader breathless.

This is an extremely courageous book which touches on what is perhaps the most perplexing and important issue of our time – where we have come from as humankind, what we are doing to ourselves and our planet in so many different realms from the psychological to the ecological, and what impact our conduct may be having on other life forms in the universe and their contemporary and future relationships with us. It dares to strip away the mantles of deliberate social, political and economic miasma that have dogged humanity since its inception, concealed the truth of our being and resulted in our present state of self-imposed pseudo religious ignorance and moral confusion. Neil Gould has dared to say that the Emperor has no clothes on. He invites his readers to listen to their intuitive reasoning when addressing these profound issues and to consider seriously the previously unthinkable notions that we are not alone in the universe nor at the top of the food chain, to accept that alternative energies are indeed available in a planet polluting itself to death with toxic hydrocarbon based fuels and to come terms with the fact that a more spiritually aware and advanced world collaborating on vital national and international issues rather than fighting over them, will ultimately prove to be a vastly improved, healthier, more productive, optimistic and happier place in which to live.

Like Neil Gould, Douglas McClure, was also born of UK stock and educated in South Africa. He studied politics, philosophy and economics at the University of Michigan, USA, and concluded post graduate studies in the UK and South Africa. He lectured in the Department of International Relations at the University of the Witwatersrand and lectured on strategic studies in the Department of Political Science at the University of Cape Town. After ten years in radio and television he worked at Cabinet level in the South African government serving three Presidents and three Cabinet ministers. He served as part of the team on the declassification of the South African ballistic missile and atomic bomb programmes, compiled the President's Council Report on Economic Literacy in South Africa and lectured at the South African Naval Staff College for twenty-two years. He also worked as part of the support team at the constitutional negotiations in the early 1990s to create a more democratic constitutional dispensation in South Africa and is currently a serving member of the Exopolitics Institute in Hawaii dedicated to creating a more accurate and broader understanding of the origins of humankind and its future prospects. He divides his time between South Africa and the UK.

Douglas McClure MA

INTRODUCTION

The Humans of this world who push the boundaries by innovation, risk and sheer tenacity without fear of consequences make way for the rest of us. I call these pioneers 'Water Humans'. Many are described as being symptomatic of ADD/ ADHD. Those who live in their shadow, or those who simply will not allow change, I call the 'Oil Humans'. The Water Humans perpetuate evolution. Water humans have supercharged minds, caring hearts and high intellect to allow humankind to cope with the speed of technical progress. Man's potential has been stifled by 'Oil Humans' entrenched in religious institutions, rogue shadow governments and financial institutions. They have painted illusions into our reality, in the interests of geopolitical control.

Water and oil do not mix. Whilst the oil rises to the surface, in reality the water holds it in place. The broader the base for water, the more oil can be supported. Water moves faster than oil and water permeates into smaller cracks and finds new avenues that the oil simply cannot. Water falls wildly over the edge of mountains cascading downwards, vigorously emitting its presence as spray and mist. Oil is slowly pumped out of the ground, a viscous, black and dirty material. It pollutes and traps nature's gems, when let loose.

This book is my journey. The world as experienced through an ADHD brain, from childhood until adulthood. I have ADHD. I could not function at school. I had several 'out-of-this-world' experiences with different types of extra-terrestrial beings. This journey took me from Africa, Europe to China. I have met many like-minded ADHD people though my interface with different forms of conscious beings, which have steered me along my sojourn.

The book is serious fun, daring adventure, and meaningful interaction with extra-terrestrials. I tell it just the way it happened. It would have been unthinkable that I would ever have embarked on this journey, let alone write a book. I could not concentrate for more than three minutes in any direction as a young man, yet here is the proof of who I am.

I have finally found peace within the new political science called Exopolitics, the study of the key individuals, political institutions and processes associated with extraterrestrial life. My cosmic brain allows me see through the cracks, a requirement of anyone who aims to challenge the worldview.

I thank Dr Michael Salla PhD and Angelika Whitecliff for founding the Exopolitics Institute in 2005. I thank Paola Harris M.Ed, Dr Rebecca Hardcastle PhD, Manuel Lamiroy Lic. Juris, SA and once again Dr Salla and Angelika Whitecliff for founding/teaching the Exopolitics Certification Program, which is one of several programs within the Exopolitics institute.

"Conventional wisdom is always wrong"

Chapter 1

Borne Into Chaos

> **FOR USE BY WHITE PERSONS**
>
> THESE PUBLIC PREMISES AND THE AMENITIES THEREOF HAVE BEEN RESERVED FOR THE EXCLUSIVE USE OF WHITE PERSONS.
>
> By Order Provincial Secretary
>
> **VIR GEBRUIK DEUR BLANKES**

Apartheid in South Africa

My very first memories of any ADD-related event must have been around 1960, when I was six years old. We lived in a house in Durban, South Africa, at the height of the Apartheid *(separation of population by race)* era, when to be black was to be "something else" and the white man reigned supreme. The Boer *(Afrikaans farmer of*

Dutch descent) was nothing less than celestial. We had just moved into a new house. In the garden was a "water well", with an attached bucket and rope. I remember the garden was a little paradise, with flowers and exotic fruit trees in the front garden. The scent of mango and papaya filled the air, scenting the days with South Africa's unique perfume. There were grape vines at the back of the house and an old grape press and wine barrel rested against the wall. The grapes were black and had that homegrown flavor to them. The skins were tough and the inside would squirt into your mouth. After making a sour face, I would spit out the skin and savor the tang of the juice. The tang was electric and sent a shiver down my body. My brain loved this type of electric stimulus.

At that time my sister Andrea was just a baby in her carrycot. Little did the world know that she would grow up to save many a child from going to prison or from dropping out of school. She would become one of the world experts on ADD/ADHD. A person you could rely on, a person whom the establishment could not silence or put down.

One night my cousin from Johannesburg flew in on a Viscount propeller airplane. It must have been around Christmas time because it was from her that I learned about 'decorations', dressing trees with streamers and dazzling materials. That night I went to sleep enjoying the thoughts of the ***de-co-ra-ti-ons*** and the fact that I had learned an adult word, a long word that grownups use.

That same night, I had my first intense, supernatural dream. I have had many since, but this first one remains as vivid as that Christmas night. In the dream, I saw a large tree outside our front door. It bore fruit shaped like red peppers but they were a dull brown color. I had the urge to pop them and as I did, they made a nerve wrenching popping sound. Soon, all the fruit were popping inside my head.

They all popped without me touching them and I could not run away or escape the sound. The sound seemed intent on driving me mad. It buried itself deeper than just in my head, reverberating in my nerves and I could not snap out of it. I woke up feeling as though I had been shot in the head. The echoes of the sound irritated me and haunted me through to the next day.

Thinking back now, I recall the rough shadowy shapes of observers who were standing below the tree, watching. It is from this point that I developed a facial tic obviously related to a new induced hyperactivity. The mainstream doctors, psychologists and psychiatrists gave me different versions of what was happening to me. At this time, ADD was not the accepted condition it is today, and doctors would not take the dream into account when examining me. Even today they are trained by institutions to think inside the box or face ridicule. For me, the dream and my condition are irrefutably linked. In dreams since then, I have awoken with heightened awareness and other abilities, more of which later.

After this first dream, often at night I began to see patterns of black specks covered in a bright bubble, which appeared when the room went dark. I still see them to this day. I cannot convey how I knew that these dots had something to do with the life force of my living mother. Her essence and expressions are encapsulated within these dots. I began to understand that consciousness and the physical body can be separated.

From this time of my life onward, I can recall how the electric hyperactivity crept in and how it started to shape my character. I have no way to medically describe how my mind was working, but for sure, I recall how the uncontrollable impulses to talk, tic and play were affecting me. Anywhere where there was a sensitive muscle,

I would engage it with a twitch in the opposite direction. Eyelids, facial muscles, tensing of back muscles until they went into spasm. I was a walking mass of hyperactivity, and people noticed.

From the tics it progressed to not walking on the cracks of the pavement. At times if I touched one part of my arm I had to touch the other in the same place. Walking past a pole, I would have to come back and walk around the pole the other way. Obsessive-compulsive behaviors, most of which I became able to control as time went on. The pent-up frustration was such that I felt like I was in a bus queue, with my feet glued to the floor as everyone else passed me to board the bus. I did not realize that the frustration was nothing more than compressed files, holding new abilities that I had yet to learn to operate.

On the positive side, I loved to play with my nursery school friends and neighbors. Games were fun and I had the most vivid imagination. I could create amazing worlds in which I'd play for hours and I could open the way for my friends to come into my world and enjoy a day with me.

I had many a fascination for strange things, things as simple as a pop-a-two ice cream. It had two sticks and you could separate them into two ice creams. White walls fascinated me; you could take your crayons and scribble on the walls of your house. The consequences were a telling off, but that seemed to fade into the distance and search for excitement seemed to grow stronger and stronger as time went on.

"Rock a bye baby on the treetop
You know we are here,
When the peppers they pop
Until we are finished,
This will not stop

*Your world is trapped
So we engineer a new crop"*

'Star Seeds' by Neil Gould

Chapter 2

The New Neighborhood

From Left to Right: Peter, Ricky, Neil and Andrea (Neil's sister) circa 1964.

The rest of my time at that house was quite uneventful, notwithstanding the fact that I was growing up and the tics were not releasing their hold on me. The internal eruptions would at times be so bad that I had to stop walking and carry out my rituals behind a door or in secret somewhere, no matter where I was, in town, school or wherever.

I was around nine years old when we moved to another house in Ocean Way, Durban North. This time I had moved into a real wild paradise. A neighborhood where there were kids for me to play with, where I could compete and challenge and grow up.

It was a house where I would face another supernatural event where a capsule was planted in my mind, releasing information as time went on, and super maturing certain parts of my brain into higher levels of consciousness. I will explain this further in the next chapter. It was this time of my life that my disposition would start to irritate some people around me. I can actually remember my thought processes from this time and I can compare them to the way other kids processed information. One thing was for sure, that I was only 'here' half the time. The rest of the time I was simply 'not here'. The 'not here' was a matrix or template of where I would like to be and embraced all the fantasies that a kid would want. The 'here' was a life of conflict, bumping into people's comfort zones and receiving lashings from my father's belt when my overactive brain caused me to misbehave. If I was told to do something, the instruction was clear, but the ADD brain then slid off into the 'not here', and the fantasy world took over. It was in this other world that I felt fine, a world of dreams, with cowboys, jungles, and adventure. I knew that the serious part of life was just too serious.

An example of my brain getting me into trouble is when I'd be told not to upset my sister. The uncontrollable urge was there to taunt and see how far I could push her. Once she got to the stage of 'The Warning', that she would tell Mom, or lash out, I'd have to threaten or create new methods to avoid trouble and keep the status quo. This state of mind takes the adrenalin to a new level. Knowing I was teetering on the edge of a lashing, yet unable to stop, felt kind of good. I learned that excitement was an absolute reward for the brain; it was the propellant. After a while as with any addiction, the brain begins to control you and you have to learn to control the brain, otherwise you are in serious conflict with society. That is the point of departure where most kids fall through the net and into the hands of the law, or into the grasp of substance abuse. From an early age I learned to strike the balance between feeding my brain the excitement it craved, yet not falling off the edge. I had several close calls though. I began to meet all the kids in the neighborhood. Across the road was Peter Morris, next door to him was Ricky Germaine and his sister little Anne. On the corner was the bully Ivan Rotten and across the road from him was David Edwin with Brian Hamley as his neighbor. A band of normal kids, all ready for a good deal of fun. Amidst all this, there was Mrs. Butler, a lonely and frightening woman. She was mad, huge and dangerous. Finally, the Kochs, a large family of German immigrants. The father was a violent alcoholic.

Peter Morris was a football fanatic. We were 10 years of age and he would drive me nuts. I liked my morning sleep but Peter would insist on banging me on the head with his football to wake me up. I hated football. I hated *sport*, but there was no place to hide from him. A great kid but so hyperactive that I felt like a tortoise. Peter understood the power of being 'not here'. Other kids would play for a while before getting bored, but Peter and I would go to the movies and re enact the entire film in our garden. I must tell you that I was not on earth when playing these games. If we saw a film on Tarzan, either he or I would *become* Tarzan, completely lost in our jungle surroundings. The games intensified and new props were required to keep up the adrenalin. If it took swinging from a tree 50ft up, so be it. If it took throwing a sand clod at a car that we decided was an elephant, so be it. If it took jumping of a cliff into the river, we would jump off the roof of the Kaya, a small house in the garden where black Zulu servants lived. Once, six of us kids were on the Kaya roof. At different parts of the roof you were either higher or lower to the ground. It was interesting to see which kid jumped and from which height. Peter and I jumped from almost bone-breaking heights. The others who were very relaxed sort of kids either hung first by their hands before falling or dropped off the roof where the ground was closest. For Peter and I, the thrill of looking down, the thrill of the fall and the smashing of our feet, then hands on the ground was amazing. The attention we got, the high we received in our brains made it a delight.

I guess you can deduce that if you line up a bunch of kids and set a dangerous challenge, the ADD/ADHD kids will be the ones at the front of the line. Many people are ADD to a degree, but when it starts to affect others or to be a danger to yourself, that is when you receive the label of ADHD.

We come in the night;
Not to give you a fright
To bury the knowledge capsule,
In your brain
You become Homo Noeticus,
Humanity can thrive again

'Seeding' by Neil Gould

Chapter 3

A Real Out-Of This-World Experience
Or
Society Would Tell Me I Imagined It

The Being; Interdimensional Manipulator

I have demonstrated that the ADHD brain needs feeding with stimulation. It creates apparent chaos as part of the solution. But do not for one minute believe that everything you read or hear about ADD or ADHD people are lies or fantasies. I hope that sharing my experiences will create a wider understanding of this condition and dispel the myths.

Shortly after moving into the house in Ocean Way, I developed an unexplainable fear of the dark. This was serious. I would never open a cupboard at night or leave a single part of my body uncovered from my sheets. My father spent time talking to me about the fear being irrational. He would open cupboards and show me nothing was there. These lessons were scary because they were done at night, the time that was most fearful to me. To be left alone or not have someone lay next to me would mean I could not sleep. Nights became my enemy, my worst fear. The demons were hidden there. I was aware of something, something that was masked and hidden from me. I had nights where I would experience something the doctors called temporal paralysis or sleep paralysis [1]. I would feel a heavy pressure on my chest. I was awake but unable to move, frozen or paralyzed.

One night I awoke feeling as calm as a cucumber. This was unheard of. My eyes were closed but I was awake. I had never in all my life felt this kind of peace. No fear, just a feeling of someone there that cared deeply for me. I sensed this very clearly and decided to bravely open my eyes. There was a low misty glowing light in the room. Standing right next to me was a hooded person in a brown robe, perhaps only four feet in height. I felt that the being was feminine, but there was no way to really know. She began to communicate with me, not in words but in a mind-to-mind connection, a sudden rush of knowledge at once. It was as though she emitted a multidimensional pattern to me, or implanted my brain with a knowledge capsule. I closed my eyes in acceptance of her. She was still there when I opened them again five minutes or so later. She was now standing by the door, still peering at me and giving off a concentrated information package. It is hard to convey in words what she told me. The information was exciting and gave meaning as to why I am here and what my potential in this world is. It was spiritual and it was real, I was not in a hypnogogic state, I was not imagining things, I was not next to a transformer or electromagnetic power junction. The proof is in the results and the effect on my life today and the marvelous out of this world experiences that happened to me. Try to understand that the interface with this being was very physical yet dimensional in that, there were years of input from her in what might have been just minutes of time. The whole room was encased in a glow of conscious energy. I still feel close to "her" as I write this book. Her answers are already there, before I have to ask the question. It is as though the capsule has a time-release mechanism, releasing more information from her over the years as and when I need it. I have felt her presence often when in a dangerous situation, and suddenly received the knowledge and sense of calm needed to keep myself safe. Many people have their own rationalizations and explanations for my experiences. Personally, I believe she was a dimensional manipulator. These are beings that treat our genes in the same way doctors treat our illnesses or implant new organs. The creator created us, the doctors looked after us, and the dimensional manipulators upgrade us.

One of the most controversial people in the field of Exopolitics is Mary Rodwell RN, Founder and Principal of the Australian Close Encounter Resource Network. (ACERN) Born in the United Kingdom, she migrated to Australia in 1991.Below is an excerpt from Mary's website (http://www.acern.com.au/), which is striking and I find commonality with my own experiences in some cases:

> *"Mary's research records testimony from small children even younger than two years old, who speak of experiences on a spacecraft. One eight year old described a 'downloading' of information from the extraterrestrials, articulated by her as 'knowledge bombs', i.e. Complex data conveyed through mental images and concepts, which seem to create a 'heightened consciousness level.' Research has shown the 'Star Children' exhibit a maturity and wisdom beyond their years, awareness and connection to spiritual realms.*
>
> *Mary's research shows while many 'Star Children' sometimes called 'Indigos,' have telepathic abilities, and are spiritually awakened and describe seeing 'Beings of Light' the main difference is that 'Star Children' have recollections of encounters with extraterrestrial beings and of being taken aboard extraterrestrial spaceships.*
>
> *Mary's research also explores the evidence from scientific, medical, psychological, and historical perspective to support what she believes is a 'genetic' engineering program, which is part of an 'upgrading' of homo sapiens, and creating a paradigm shift in human consciousness, which these children demonstrate. Data suggests such children are being altered and transformed on many levels through extraterrestrial encounters and with some genetic engineering. Mary's research includes some of the latest DNA research which could qualify how this up-grading could and may occur".*

Some ADHD could very well be a manifestation of the dimensional manipulators. For ADHD people, it is hard to fit into the world. From an early age, the condition causes us to break the rules, rebel and think outside the box. Those of us who can understand and embrace ADHD have gone on to invent the technologies that quicken the pace of development, to push the boundaries and to let humankind progress away from war, greed and hidden knowledge. For those ADHD people who have had supernatural experiences, it is important to let the world know about the dimensional manipulators and to take away the ridicule so that the future will progress. Not just for the privileged twenty percent of the world population, I mean the sodden eighty percent, who are trodden on and deprived of power, medicine, education, food and life.

By experiencing these spiritual events, it becomes hard to ignore wrongness and harder still to see that some of your friends have not evolved past the dollar or their own ego. You see members of your communities doing good deeds, because they really care. Others do so, simply because they can afford to, or because it results in recognition and fame within their community.

The knowledge capsule enables me to understand dramatic current events, those lights being reported flying around in the sky, a subject that is swept under the carpet for fear of ridicule. I can see through the cracks, I have to, in order to assist in any events that are extra terrestrial in nature.

> *Why is this subject swept under the carpet? Air traffic control see them on radar, our military secretly call them fastwalkers, (slowwalkers are satellites). They are filmed over our airports, nuclear installations [2] and cities. Do we need to live in the dark? We are in the dark and kept there by the Oil Humans.*

The incident with the hooded being, when reported to my mother, was passed off as it being she who came into the room. I suspect this was to keep me sane and not stoke up the fire. It is an understandable reaction. A week later, I had terrible nosebleeds, followed by sinus troubles. These events continued on and off for weeks, months and years.

> *"The first task in addressing that question is moving away from literal thinking; this star or that star. They may come from another dimension. One shaman asked them where they're from and they answered, nowhere and everywhere. They might come from a star system. Who knows?"*
> Interview with Dr. John E. Mack, October 2002

Chapter 4

Breaking the Rules
Or
Do As I Say, Not As I Do

In any civilized world, there are boundaries. In our neighborhood, there were rules and boundaries set up by our parents, in relation to our unique environment.

Rule One: Do not go into the bushveld, it is full of snakes.

Rule Two: Do not play with matches, it is dangerous.

Rule Three: Behave yourself at all times.

Rule Four: Be careful of Mrs. Butler, she is mad so keep away from her house.

Rule Five: Look out for the bully Ivan Rotten and keep away.

Our neighborhood was on the border of the bush, which was an unexplored paradise for kids. Snakes were a common sight in our garden. Mr. Haze, the local snake catcher, would come periodically to clean up the snakes. He would wear leather boots that went up to his knees and carried special poles, which were the tools of his trade.

Mr. Haze was very possessive of his poles so whilst he was gearing up and his back was turned, Peter or I would make a grab for the poles, just to squeeze the pole handle and see what happened. We would both make a grab and end up squabbling over the pole. Mr. Haze would turn around with a snarl on his face and just out of the line of sight of my mother; he'd whip back the poles, hoping to catch one of our hands.

Mr. Haze used to check the garden at one end and we would be playing our game of snake catching at the other end, using branches as improvisations for the poles. Would you believe it, Peter turned over a slate and underneath was an adder. Instead of calling Mr. Haze, we decided to play a game of snake catching. We tried all sorts of ways to prod and poke the adder to move it into the open. It was a boring snake, it hardly moved. Our African servant passed by on the way to water the lawn. Upon seeing what we were doing he pushed us aside whilst he clubbed the poor snake with his knobkerrie *(a wooden hand held Zulu fighting stick with a wooden ball at one end)*. Mr. Haze saw this and went ballistic at us, citing that we were naughty and playing a very dangerous game and could get ourselves killed. He could have gotten 10 cents per foot from the Durban Snake Park if he had delivered the snake alive. He played that he was concerned for our safety, or was his anger because we did a better job than he at finding the snakes?

The other kids were in the background, well away from the snake. I began to realize that Peter and I were different. First rule broken.

In the group, Ricky Germaine was our hero. He was the all rounder, stronger than all of us. He always led the way and we looked up to him. He was an amiable, well-balanced kid, with a face full of freckles. He told us that he had freckles because when he was very young the flies pooped on his face. Ricky went on in later years to become a well-known surfer.

He had a very calm temperament, but he was the one to come up with pranks and it was he who'd encourage us all to carry them out. His sister Anne was a darling; she was kind, rotund, very friendly and always hung out with the boys. A real little tomboy.

We would go round to Ricky's house and the first hurdle was always a moan from his mother. She was huge and I mean huge. She always seemed to have a go at him about something. My mind cannot recall what she said, but I used to watch the rolls of fat behind her knees as she walked across the kitchen, scolding Ricky. The floorboards would creak as she passed by and the servant's metal dishes would shake on the precariously built wooden kitchen table. It was like I was watching a film, not reality, as again, I was 'not there'. The wobbles of the fat fascinated me, wondering what they looked like further up her dress, and if the color of her skin was whiter than that which was visible. She paced back and forth, lecturing Ricky on something or other. She bent down to pick something up and the thighs were now visible, huge fat rolls that wobbled and did not look like a thigh. There were muffles in my eardrum that grew louder and louder and along came a scream from Anne, "Watch it, she is talking to you!".

My ADHD brain gets me into trouble again. The conversation had apparently turned to me in that I was asked why I was a bad influence on her son by going into the bush. At that point my eyes had been focused on this whale-like polka (thigh) and I got caught.

Old Neil is a dirty bastard, go home. She erupted and I did not know why my attention had wondered off like that. I was afraid to go back there for months.

We would always give Ivan's house a clear miss when walking to David Edwin's. Two years older than me, David was a tall freckly boy who at every opportunity would put his hands down the front of his pants. He would do it unconscious of any of us being around. He told us he was practicing something for when he was older. Was he ADD? No not really, just a lad who had a father who swore at everyone and who never let this poor kid touch anything. In effect, he had no father but he had a good time. His dad used to make model cars, trains, and planes and fly them. They had this model train set in the loft of their house and we would play with it whilst David's dad was out. David's secret was that when Dad was out we would be in. The train set and its scenery were over 50 ft long. It had bridges, foliage and farms. We were in another world. Brian Hamley was the 'chips' man, the one to stand by the window and check that Dad was not coming home. And so it started, we each had turns driving the train. The trick was to slow down at the corners and 'Do Not Lean On The Table' was the rule. No doubt you can guess who drove the trains off their track and who leant on the table. A part of the track collapsed as the table went down from Peter and I reaching over trying to nudge a train carriage. Peter slipped and grazed his chin. It took a frantic hour to reconstruct everything, with Brian keeping chips and Barry, David's older brother, helping us. I noticed how nervous David was, terrified that his father would come home before we finished. We succeeded in putting the railway all back together in time, but this was yet another rule broken.

Chapter 5

A Black Angel saves our White Skins

It was playtime again. Ricky had this idea that we all go over to my house because he'd thought of a new game, 'Took Tookie'. My house was best because it was near the bush.

The point of the game was to knock on someone's door and then run fast. Ricky and Brian took the easy dare. They would knock on our timid neighbor's door and we would all hide behind the wall. Ricky and Brian sneaked up, bending low, went up to the front door, pressed the bell and ran. They took cover with us. Three times they rang the doorbells and retreated. The occupant was frustrated, as she looked left and right. We all giggled together in delight.

The level of thrill was there but as usual, we had to go a step further. Ricky said that Peter and I had to ring Mrs. Butler's bell. Well let me tell you about her.

In the beginning, she was sort of ok. You would be invited in and this scary sasquatch-shaped woman would ask you to put your hand in the cookie jar and take a cookie or sweet. Her low rough voice growled, "Take one, take one only". She would push the jar towards you hoping you would take two then your hand would get stuck in the jar. When this happened, her eyes turned mean and we would run. One time Brian's hand was still in the jar and we had to wrestle him away from her. A year later she went totally mad and would parade down the road in her nightclothes during the day. Her house seemed evil; it had eyes and a mouth by fluke of the design of the door and windows. The whole neighborhood was wary of her; the postman threw the mail onto her balcony. He had had encounters of the weird kind.

What a rush, Peter and I were to knock on Mrs. Butler's door. The mood changed as we neared her house. Brian and Dave were relieved that it was not them to do the deed. Brian was shaking, Ricky was egging Peter and I on. The thrill was there, the adrenalin pumping, the brain eager for its fix. Peter was nervous and I was facing the biggest initiation ceremony into gang hood. No way out. I didn't want to do it but Ricky kept egging us on, saying it was nothing and he'd do it all by himself, except that it was not his turn. We procrastinated as much as we could and took cover behind the wall. We had to get down the pathway, across the front garden, unseen, to reach her front door. She was often seen peeping out her window, shooting an evil stare at whoever was around. It could happen at any time. If we were caught then that was it. It was a rule to stay away. If Ricky's mother heard about his, I could very well end up with a roll of fat bashing my lughole. If I succeeded then I would be a senior member of the crew. Peter and I checked it out carefully. We decided on a 45-degree attack to the door from the front corner of the garden, so she could not see us from her favorite chair by the left hand window. It was not a good sign that every now and then, Brian was signaling us to hurry up. He was exposing his position. Ricky gave us that look of assurance, which you could bank on. We were very near the door, just a few yards to go. Now we were standing exposed on the balcony and Peter pressed the doorbell and ran. He slipped on the doormat but regained his stature and we bolted in the same direction we came. Brian was trembling like a leaf. My heart was pumping pure adrenalin. I was near heaven, no consequences in my mind at all. Nice feeling. Nice feelings came with big risk. No reaction from Mrs. Butler; we had to give it a second shot. Everyone gave their pennyworth on how to do it and what to do next. It was dangerous but that was where the energy came from. At this point there were no rules, no parents, no school, no responsibility and no consequences. The only thing that I was chasing was the high.

We crept towards the front door one more time. Peter in front and myself right behind him. It seemed to take an hour to walk 10 yards. We had arrived on the balcony. Peter stopped, but I could not understand why. Once I'd realized, it was too late. He had seen first that the door was slightly ajar by two inches. In a split second this huge monster hurled out of the door and grabbed Peter by the top of his arm. We screamed, she growled, her eyes were like lasers cutting into my mind, my bottom lip went numb; I had bitten it. Peter was being dragged into the cave and was on his back reaching for me, screaming like he was in the jaws of the dragon. It was all in slow motion. I reached for him and secured a grip on his shirtfront but by now he was halfway into the house. She managed to tug both of us to the door. I had to let go. I could not take the thought of her mincing him up with a cleaver or tying him to a bedpost and eating him. Those were the rumors. The screams went on. The rest of the group stood, frozen and then ran. I was paralyzed, half wanting to be a hero and half wanting to follow them. The door was shut. The screams of terror continued and I heard poor Peter being slapped. I could now hear Mrs. Butler's screams; they were more frightening than ever. Suddenly her front door ripped open and I saw an angel from heaven grab Peter and run out of the house. It was one of our picannins *(pre pubic black kids during the apartheid era, today it is a derogatory word)*. Every house had a Kaya where the African servants lived and most of them secretly kept kids or family members cramped inside. The Zulu kids were known as picannins and in the Apartheid era they were always there, behind a tree or bush watching us white people, play. They were not allowed to mix but they were like pixies, knowing the rules of the wild and knowing how to survive. One Zulu kid had been shadowing us and had seen the incident. Spiritual law dictated that he sneak into the house of Mrs. Butler and grab Peter. He had used his bush hunting instincts and stealth to get into the house, get proximity to Peter, snatch him from harm and run at great risk to his life. He dropped Peter in front of me and I took him and ran. By that time the Zulu kid was already out of sight. He had to be. He had to stay hidden. He did not have a dreaded "Dompass" *(special pass to enter the White zone)* to allow him into the white man's city to live with his mother. He was an invisible hero. Always there, yet always unseen. If it weren't for him, I don't know what gruesome fate would have befallen Peter. Rule Four broken.

Chapter 6

The Third World War

Another day passed. Another rule broken and it seemed normal. My knowledge capsule continued to remind me of its presence. I had developed increased perceptions, or an enabled second sight of some sort. I was too young to put any of this into any perspective. At that age, everything seemed normal. However, my parents often mentioned that my vivid imagination was a little out of order, reporting animals in the garden that did not exist.

In the summer1964, there was a lot of activity next to my house. A huge bulldozer had arrived. We did not know what it was for, but it was left outside my house. Peter and I began by playing on it and trying to figure out how to start it. It was locked, but was nevertheless a great toy. That afternoon, a group of Africans under the control of the white supervisor started to move into the bush, ripping up trees and leveling an area. They were going to build a school, later to become Beachwood High School. The digging stopped at 5.00pm and we went to explore. There were these mounds of red sand and in places it had lumped together as sand clogs. If you threw one it was like a grenade. As it hit the ground it popped and spattered red sand everywhere like a gory explosion. It was time for a game. Anne, Ricky and I on the side of the British and Brian, Dave and Peter were the Gerrys. We threw clods at each other and it was wonderful, it was World War Three. For Peter and me, it really was World War Three. We could see our Spitfires flying over and bombing the Gerrys and the German Stukas were machine-gunning us. By now as usual, the game was really just Peter and me as the others had become bored. As the game intensified, we needed more action, more adrenaline and more targets. What the hell, the Kochs next door were real live Germans! Mutter, the big fat mother, was washing the clothes of her 6 kids; Dietland, Wolfgang, Renate, Goodren and I cannot remember the names of the others. We put the clogs down and Peter said he saw 10 Gerrys in her house. He picked up a stick and machine-gunned them. I could see his spit flying from his mouth as he did it. I liked the sound so I also gave my own version of a ratattatat. I got 3 of them but Peter said we had to blow up the whole house, as there was a nest of Gerry's planning to mortar us. This was serious. I had already slipped into 'not here' and I was not coming out of it. I was excited and shaking. What would happen if we did not get 'em first? How would we blow them up? Peter said, "Easy. Let's stack some grenades in a pile along the back wall and then we can launch an attack." We must have piled up over 100 sand clods the size of my fist that day. Peter gave the signal, "*Himmel! Donner und Blitz!*" as quoted in our war comics and we threw the clods over the wall. We ran from stack to stack, reloading our arsenal and launching wave after wave of missiles. The clods landed on the roof, in their courtyard, on their driveway, on their front lawn. The Gerrys position was covered in red exploding sand, a dreadful mess. We had killed off the whole battalion. Now the dream ended with a shock. The game was over, now for the consequences. For the life of me, I cannot understand why I would do such a thing.

The whole neighborhood was gathered outside the Koch's, as Mutter's screams had attracted everyone. Ivan the bully was there too, so Peter and I stood together, watching from my house next door. In her German accent Mutter was screaming and shouting, "Who do zis sing to uz?!"

She was ranting and all the neighbors were puzzled. We sat with blank poker faces. Mrs. Koch looked at Peter and me and snarled, "It vas you two".

"No", we retorted, " No, NO!" "Zen vy are you covered vis der seme sand dat ish on mine house?" With that Peter ran like hell. Ivan the bully targeted me and chased me but I got into our house, too quick for him to catch me. After this, a long meeting was held between my parents and Peter's, culminating in the long task of cleaning the roof, garden and everywhere in Mutter's house where the bombs had landed. The strange thing is that I do not have a clue as to why or how I could have done such a thing. I was chasing a high, stimulating my brain. ADHD is all about pushing the boundaries, breaking the laws of order and satisfy the burning requirements of an ADHD or ADD brain. We were in trouble again.

The war was over but the battle was only just beginning. Life at home was a problem for my parents. I was not performing in school. I was not doing homework. The point is that I simply did not remember to and when asked to do it, it interfered with my state of well being. My desires were to play, to feed this ADHD mind of mine with excitement. It literally brushed away everything and anything to do with school, which I hated so much.

This brought me into my first real conflicts at home, where my mother went crazy and my father only knew that a lathering with the belt made him feel better. My self-esteem started a dangerous slide downwards. People at that time did not understand the ADHD condition existed; let alone treat it. I began to recall those shadows that stood under the popping tree in my dream. I developed a fear of going to bed. I was blocking many an incident from my conscious mind. I still do so today, frequently staying up all night rather than going to bed.

A few weeks later I developed an abscess on my gum and was put under a very light general anesthetic to remove it. The anesthetic put me into a twilight state and I saw very clearly an image of my father holding my arm. He shouted, "Hold on" in a very stern voice. We were being released from a curved metallic vehicle and we had to step off the edge. It was only about ten feet in diameter. I cannot forget the echo of my father's fearful words, "Hold on" as we disembarked. Here was a man that believed nothing I ever said. The incident was buried deep within his subconscious. He passed away in 2002; he remained a non believer till the very end. I never had the chance to tell him about this, since this memory although always in my mind, was held back for whatever reason.

"Like any new shoe, it will hurt for a while

The knowledge capsule will settle,

Enhance your spiritual profile

You will look from within and

You will look from outside

You will expose man's evil, far and wide"
"Maverick", by Neil Gould

Chapter 7

Us vs. Them
Or
Antics and impulse

Peter and I spent more time together than with the rest of the bunch. We would talk for hours. In most cases, it was a pissing contest. He had a stronger friend or his dad was richer and so on. We sat on my steel framed jungle gym, trading insults out of boredom. When things went quiet, the tongues got sharper. In fact, most of the time, our banters were exchanged at the very same moments. We were interrupting each other all the time. Neither ever listened. Each jibe had to be stretched into fantasy in order to outdo the others boast. Next it was that he had a cousin who was a scientist, so therefore he must be right. Suddenly I had an uncle who was a chief scientist. We got to the point where the atmosphere turned nasty and unless we found something else to do we would end up parting ways for the day. Two ADHDs on the loose in hyperactive mode? Peter claimed that he could shoot the head off a match from 100ft away when he was on the farm. Well we did not have any guns but we certainly could get hold of matches. Out of this creation, we were able to use cotton thread and tie pins to hold the matches in place, cut a long papaya leaf off the tree and presto, a blowgun. So what can we shoot now?

In South Africa, each household invariably had a gardener who was male, a cook who was female and perhaps another helper for the cleaning and washing. At the back of each house was a Zulu Kaya, living quarters for the servants. Basic digs, with 2 rooms and a latrine that consisted of a hole in the ground with a flushing mechanism. Next to the Kaya were the clotheslines where the servants would hang the washing. The female servants were very loving and warm Zulus, patient and fantastic with kids. They wore a white uniform and a headscarf called a Duk. There was no getting away from the huge rump, which beset every female Zulu who lived with you. Its growth was due to a mix of genetics and a huge appetite for sugar, bread, mielie meal (*ground corn*) and medumbes (*type of potatoes*). We would watch them disappear in and out sight as they walked down the rows of clotheslines, hanging out the sheets to dry. Every now and then we would see them bend down into the basket to pick up another piece of washing to place on the line. I felt like a lioness, stalking its prey. Peter and I did not have to discuss what the target was for our new blow pipes. We had to creep up and get into position where we could blow our darts out and not be seen. What better target than the huge rear of a Zulu lady. We were now in Brazil. We always had a machete, or Panga, and we would pretend to cut away the reeds and vines until we got to the target. In this case a kind of wild animal. We had to blow our poison darts at the animal fast and we had to do it a few times to be sure they got the right dose. As it happens the Zulus love singing, a very calming effect on babies, but we were seasoned hunters now and the target had to be hit. We crept up and hid behind the zinc-plated tub. We aimed our darts at the rear of the animal and blew. The result was a series of continuous darts, which ploughed into the rear of two of the servants. Their lullabies turned into shrieks as they realized they had been hit and they frantically pulled out the darts out, completely bewildered. Noticing that the invader was not a bee or hornet, it could only have been one thing. We were chased and reported to our parents. Once again we were in trouble, but with no realization that what we were doing to others was wrong. Later in the day we teamed up and thought what can we do with the matches? Oh yes, lets go to the bush where they are building the Beachwood school and see what's up. Maybe make a campfire and enjoy the creation of flames from a mere box of Lion Matches.

The air was dry, the grass was so dry and it was hot as hell. We walked into the edge of the bush and there we saw the school nearly fully built. We decided to try to light a piece of grass and then put it out quick. This we did. The grass erupted into a flame, which spread rapidly. We both got a shock and stamped the flame out with our bare feet. Nobody wore shoes then. Our soles were tough. Shaking, we looked at each other and had found our entertainment for the day. What a kick we got out of the shock of watching the flames erupt so fast. It looked like gunpowder in the movies. This time we thought both of us would have our own match and light our own fire and stamp it out ourselves. The excitement was building up. I was moving from this world into my world. Gone were the consequences, gone were the interruptions, and gone was the boredom. My brain was alive; I could taste the fun to come. Peter and I each lit our own match and set fire to the dry grass, which was a lot taller than the earlier grass that we had stamped out. We dared ourselves to let the flames get bigger and then we would stamp both fires out. Great idea, except now the two fires spread 360 degrees and as we battled at one end to stamp them out they grew rapidly at the other end and yes, we were in the middle, helpless, excited before the realization grew that we had a problem on our hands here. A real whopper. I grabbed Peter and said, "Run man, run!" We galloped and holding each other's hand, jumped through the ring of flames and bolted to my house. Peter was crying. I told him not to look back. The flames were 30 foot tall and the whole side of the Beachwood perimeter was on fire, and so were the trees and the wind was blowing towards Brian Hamley's house. 20 minutes later the fire engines arrived. They plugged their hoses into the hydrants with speed and tackled the fire. A huge crowd turned up to watch. I went to the firefighter and asked him how the fire started. Peter would not come anywhere near. He watched from my garden tree house. We never discussed this again nor did we tell anyone how it happened.

"I had a terrible education. I attended a school for emotionally disturbed teachers." — Woody Allen.

"To invent, you need a good imagination and a pile of junk." — Thomas Edison.

Chapter 8

Missing time
Or
Close Encounter of the ADD kind

Another beautiful day had set in. It was a Sunday because my folks were home and my pal had come to visit me. It was one of those days where we had a phenomenon called a "Berg wind". The wind would blow from the inland African mountain range called the Drakensberg (*Dragons back*) and it would superheat. When it arrived, the temperature would jump up from an ambient 84 degrees to 105 degrees. We would recognize it every year and we would rush to any metal objects just to feel the heat. Windows had metal frames so we would lay our hands on them to feel the temperature soar. It always created a frenzy of conversation. You could almost hear the grass drying out and the spitting bugs seemed to be more active when this wind arrived. A spitting bug, to be honest, I never saw, but they existed. A blob high up on the trees and every now and then a large ping-pong ball size droplet would land on someone's head. Certain trees we knew not to sit under. Not only because of the spitting bug but there were blue headed lizards which used to scurry up and down the tree. I'm sure they were harmless, but we did not take chances.

Ricky, his little sister Anne and Peter came over. We were all sitting on our front patio or verandah as we called it. Wearing shorts, we had to be careful not to let our exposed legs touch the patio for fear of a burn. The air was very hot. Ricky had an unusual long knife. We all wanted turns to hold it. My pal Garland, a quiet lad, took the knife and carefully checked all along the blade, careful not to cut himself. Anne did not bother but she passed it to Peter. A lunatic with a knife, in no time, he was throwing it to see if the blade would peg into the ground. Each time he threw, it came nearer to my foot and at that point, Ricky took it back. Peter was jumping up and down, so hyperactive; he wanted just one more turn. Ricky said O.K. as long as he did not throw it. Finally, Peter had it all to himself and he seemed to aim it at Brian's house, and then did a mock death as though he had been stabbed in the chest. That was it. The knife was back in Ricky's sheath.

"Now," said Ricky, "Today we are going on an expedition." I asked where, as it was Sunday, Garland was being fetched at 5.00pm and I had to be around at that time too.

"I can't tell you, just follow me and you'll see" Ricky said with a grin. We were all barefoot. Our feet were hard as leather. Ricky had his knife and we all gathered some sort of weapon, a curtain pole or a garden axe. You never knew what you'd need for an expedition, but it didn't hurt to be prepared. Ricky led the way as we walked out of the house and up the road, skirting the bush. When we got to the top of the hill, Ricky said, "Come on, our parents can't see us." We walked down a hill with houses on one side and at the bottom was a concrete donga (*part concrete part natural water course*) with two huge pipes draining water into it. On the floor of the donga was a sort of green slimy algae. This looked like fun. We all took turns sliding up and down the donga. There was a dark tunnel leading from the donga, which passed underneath a highway that ran down to the north coast. The cars passed overhead. It was scary because it was dark inside, but we ran through it and on the other side the scenery had changed completely. The other side of the donga, which ran under the tunnel, emptied into a white clay gully. In the water were colored fish. Ricky jumped in and then we all followed. It was a welcome relief from the hot wind. By the time we were all in the water, it had turned white, as the clay had been stirred up.

Peter scooped a handful off the wall and shaped it into an ashtray. This was it. This was fun. We spent so much time just making things and enjoying the feeling of sliding clay off the wall of the donga. The fascination took over. It was like free plasticine, a type of putty. We made so many plates and left them to dry. Where we had scooped the white clay away from the donga wall, it revealed firmer, grey colored clay underneath. Repeatedly we got lost in time with this magic natural material. It was cool to the touch and smelled clean. We loved it, but Ricky was the leader and it was time for the expedition to move on. A few yards ahead, we came to a small thicket of trees. They had monkey ropes hanging down from them. These were natural vines and very strong. Peter and I, as usual climbed them first. Ricky noticed that our dogs had found us. My Dachshund, Parry, and Peter's Boxer, Major, had found us. They always seemed to turn up when we were heading for trouble. I guess they had an instinct to protect their owners.

Peter swung down from the tree and ran to hug the dogs. By now, everyone was swinging in the tree without incident. Once again, it was time to move on. Ricky sat us down and explained that ahead was a private orchard with fruit beyond our wildest dreams, but they had a dog-called Cherchaw. Ricky said it was mean as hell and it would tear us apart and so he had to go first to train the dog and scare it into submission. We were not allowed to see his magic act. We heard Ricky call Cherchaw and he peered over to ensure we were not around, but we were peeking. This wonderful Labrador arrived with its tail wagging and when it got to Ricky it cowered down onto its back and Ricky stroked his tummy. At this point Ricky said that we were to come along and that he had battled the dog and got its respect. We never questioned him and it seemed as kids we believed his word rather than what we had seen. I suppose it was respect. We all crept slowly into the orchard. It was a deserted house in the middle of nowhere and Ricky had obviously been here before. He knew it backwards. We ate passion fruits, mango and papaya all fresh off the vines and into our mouths. It was the mischievousness more than anything else at this point that turned us on. It was time to move on again. What a day, three exciting things, first a donga, then clay and now an orchard. The adventure was getting more interesting.

We moved on again, all of us elated and wondering what was next. Ricky told us to expect a swamp very shortly. He said it was full of bulrushes and many mangrove crabs along the bank. We saw it in the distance, and it was an eerie spectacle. There were hundreds of reeds blurting out of the landscape and a pungent smell of sulphur. Crabs scurried into their little holes, each with one claw larger than the other. Little fish braved the pool edges and the waterfowl were stabbing away. We all stared at this remarkable scene. Ricky warned that it was full of quicksand. I loved this word. I had seen many films and books about quicksand, how if you fell into it, you faced an agonizingly slow death with no chance of escape. Quicksand was exciting stuff. I asked Ricky where exactly the quicksand was and he said everywhere. Well, it didn't look like the quicksand I grew to love in my films, just plain stinking mud, so as you would expect, it was a race between Peter and me to walk into the swamp. The first few feet were fine, but it got deeper. The problem now was that Peter was almost crying and I was not sure why until I moved towards him. The dogs were barking and drowning out Ricky's voice. Peter was red faced, terrified. Each step I took towards him caused the other foot to be sucked deeper into this mud. You could hear the slurping noises from the mud, sounding like a granny slurping her bean and barley soup. The mud had us up to our groin and we were not doing ourselves any favors by moving; it just sped up the inevitable. If we stood still, we both sank, little by little. If we touched each other's hands, we would tilt but sink sideways and each movement would suck the other down. I looked into Peter's eyes and he was crying from fear. He would not answer, he was mentally gone.

Major was pawing the side of the swamp, contemplating how to jump in. He knew he could not do it. The dog was yelping, watching his master and friend in big trouble. The mud had us in a stranglehold. In my mind, the thought was, "What will happen next?" I did not think that I could be buried alive forever; this thought was not there, unlike Peter. I tried to turn and search for a way out, more concerned at Peter's state of mind at that moment. Ricky was not there, if anything that freaked me out. Anne was crying, Garland seemed to be searching for something. Slow motion set in. So did absolute clarity. Sound started to disappear and so did smell, but a pressure began to loom in my head. A mixture of cold lighter fuel and ice surged through my neurons, as if I was in the middle of an adventure film. Concern crept in, but I saw Ricky had arrived back. He had cut long lengths of the vines that we had swung on and began throwing them at us. "Grab them," he shouted. Peter was just not with it. He heard nothing, lost in his fear. I grabbed the vine. I was a good 15ft into the swamp and Peter was ahead of me by a few feet. Ricky and Garland pulled and I pulled too. Finally, I caught Peter's eye and I told him if he did not stop crying he would sink and die. That got his attention. He managed to lean towards me and got hold of my shirt. After tugging and tussling for about ten minutes, the mud slowly let go her grip. A grandmother's loud belch blurted out and we were now both on our tummies, being pulled ashore by our hero Ricky. I got out first, not noticing the next menace, about 40 monkeys taking extreme interest in us. Peter was finally dragged out and once he was on terra firma he said, "Hey that was lekker (*great* in Afrikaans slang). Let's do it again". What a twat he was, we knew it was a cover up for this huge mistake. All of us were covered in stinking mud. My sense of smell returned and so did the realization of my predicament. I recall a few minutes of shaking and a great sense of relief.

The monkeys moved in. We had followed this trail right up to the wild beach about 100 meters ahead. We could not go back, only towards the sea and it was getting dark.

We heard faint cries in the distance and wondered if we were near a sports field or something. We preferred to ignore these calls. We had to head towards the wild beach, as the monkeys were dangerous in groups. Major and Parry had encountered these monkeys before and they knew the danger. We were concerned that it was past twilight. Major charged the monkeys and they scattered towards the swamp bank area. We saw this break in the circle and ran for it, hoping we would skirt the sea which was shark infested along the Natal coast. The wild beach took us onto a man-made pebbled road, which had a very flimsy bridge over a waterway that opened onto a clearing. There to our utter shock, were my parents and Garland's parents. Faces were long and anger was high. I saw one of the boys receive a crack. Garland was ushered into the car. I was 'assisted' into the car. All hell broke loose. Obviously, our parents had been looking for us. It was 7.00pm. We were two hours late. We had been abducted by Mother Nature and distracted by a chemical rush. We had been lured by the adventure playground, where you could shape nature's material into ashtrays and plates for free. Where you could eat fruit off the vine and sink into mother earth with your friends pulling you out. It is a place that I relive every time I go to bed at night. I remember it so well and I remember how we got high on nature, so high that we lost touch with reality, no smell and no sounds, pure joy. Time was elastic and consequences once again were not part of the donga nor of the orchard experience. This was a Close encounter of the ADHD kind.

We were all severely punished and we had to endure mothers screaming at us about how worried they were and how we were naughty, you know; nothing new. We just wanted that noise to go away, which it did if you could hang in there and let the storm pass.

> "What a lesson I had.
> Mother Nature's playground
> With all its gifts and dangers
> A model of the real world
> We worked together as one
> How could we not pull through".

"In our obsession with antagonisms of the moment, we often forget how much unites all the members of humanity. Perhaps we need some outside universal threat to make us recognize this common bond. I occasionally think how our differences worldwide would vanish if we were facing an Alien threat from outside this world".

Ronald Reagan's speech to the United Nations General Assembly 42nd Assembly, 21 September 1987

Chapter 9

The crumbling of the self-esteem
Or
You cannot feel what I can see from here

This is the period of my life, at the age of 11 or 12 years old that the world began to cave in on me. If this place, Earth, is a place of learning before we ascend heavenwards, then I must have been the guinea pig. Everything was just thrown at me. My concept of "I" was meaningless, my ego – non-existent and any charge that I had left, was put out at each step of the way. Life was all about walking uphill. Later I was to learn that each step I took, prepared me for the way ahead. At this point, it was time to really put aside the Peter Pan in me. How I struggled to do so, and how I had to retreat back into that world. It was my security, otherwise what was there for me? I had upset my parents, I had upset my school and I had become an embarrassment to others. I just could not really fit in. My interests were different, hated sports and could not do the right thing and pretend, in order to conform to society's expectations. In the eyes of my father, I was a failure and told so many an occasions. He was a control freak but on the other hand very warm to people. I was not allowed near his things. Not near his camera, not near his cupboard and not near his slide projector. Under the circumstances, I guess he was being protective of his assets. My mother and he often ended up in shouting matches over me and my behavior and lack of convention. Can you blame them?

It was just one more rejection to add to the list. If not for grandparents, there would be scars. My Grandfather always came to the rescue. A Yorkshire man living in Durban was my closest ally. I could do nothing wrong in his eyes, I guess because he did not have to clean up afterwards. He was a dreamer, perhaps bi-polar as he had many bouts of depression I was later told, but nevertheless, each time I called him, he would answer saying, "Is that Neil?" It was the way he said my name. He made it glow.

My grandfather had a scrap yard in Durban and this was my Aladdin's cave. I would go there and would spend all day in the different sheds. There were barrels of brass filings, and filings from all sorts of metals, which the Zulus would strip out of any machine that he bought. I would be attracted like a magpie as the rays of the sun hit the barrels. The glow of the copper, the flash of the steel and the gold haze that reflected off the brass. Old trumpets and musical instruments on the walls and an old plane stored in the back shed awaiting the Zulus tools of destruction. I managed to take home huge batteries, Morse code units, and a hand generator, which pushed out harmless but painful volts when the handle was turned. This I loved the most. The scrap yard was my physical Peter Pan world. I had it all to myself. My grandfather never told me to leave anything alone; there was nothing I could not have. I could have the world and I did, when he was alive. One of the biggest losses of my life was when he passed over. I could make him laugh and during his sick years, it was I that prolonged his existence on this plane. I knew how to enter his mind and how to adjust the controls, which made him happy. I told him stories, which made him fall down crying in laughter. Nothing was funnier than my bottom jokes, and nothing was more rewarding than being in that moment watching him so happy. I would exist within the cracks of time whilst watching him laugh, forgetting the moment of being torn apart in front of all the school kids by a school teacher, or being whacked at the end of the day at home or being labeled as a fool or idiot. He was a barrier keeping those demons at bay.

Most kids did their homework after school. I went to school but did not do homework that often. In South Africa, we were caned for any misdemeanor. It could be one stroke with the cane or six strokes at worst. The cane left a terrible weal on the skin of the buttocks. The pain flashed through your brain and its intensity forced you to make a sound, to let out the old air and let in the new air. I was sent so many times for a caning that it was a forgone conclusion that I would encounter the cane every week; hence I didn't want to go to school. It was jail to me, it was torture, it was a strange land where people had to conform, where you could not push boundaries, where the equipment was not sophisticated enough to stimulate my active brain, where I had no chance to grow and mature. I started to see other kids similar to me in the headmaster's office, always at the brunt of punishment. I realized that some of them also did not do homework and had tics. Some later slipped even further down the ladder into drugs, stealing, violence and other non-healthy activities. I could see that some people were conformers, or they could play the game and were patient, whilst others were like me, impatient, and in need of stimulation.

Some of the parents of my friends told their kids to stay away from me. Friends were removed. People cut me off. Teachers separated me from some of the kids at the request of their parents. Who was I? What was I? Did my parents know? If they did, we did not really talk about it in any constructive way. One thing was for sure they realized that there was a problem. They thought that I was a moron because that is what I appeared to be. They had no way to know that I was suffering from extreme symptoms of ADHD. Finally, around the age of 13 or so they took me to a Child Psychologist. Verdict? Bright normal kid. BUT no mention of ADHD. Problem not solved, so another doctor put me onto tranquilizers. I became a zombie. I could not feel the zest or excitement I yearned for. All my bodily functions caved in. I threw the pills out. An interesting point about the way school affected me was the way the different subjects were contended with. Biology was always easy. It was visual, it was practical, it was scientific, and our teacher, Barry, was very meticulous in the way he taught. We respected him. Therefore, in this subject I received high grades, even if I only half studied. I knew the pulse of life. I understood it naturally. As soon as I had English or Afrikaans or Hebrew, my mind shut down. The Hebrew teacher would be ecstatic about the way Yochanan Ben Prachim came down the mountain and to tell you the truth if he pulled an ear bud out of his bottom, it would be more meaningful. What a load of absolute garbage, religious study. It meant nothing. The system of school education did not really allow for much choice of subjects. Therefore, you were stuck in the mud. Again no choice, no room to cover my interests, just a take it or leave it. Performance was based on what I had to study, not what I needed or wanted to study. Not exactly a menu dressed for choice and worse than that, if my concentration waned, it was, "Neil, off to the office my boy."

Parents please concentrate and take note.
During Afrikaans language lessons, I was so bored that I used to

visit dreamland. In one lesson, I remembered that my granddad had let me take the hand generator home. I had it in my bag. Before the next class, I very gently pulled the gizmo out of my bag and over the period of 8 minutes managed to tie the positive wire around the chair of the kid in front of me and the negative lay loose under his leg. The kid had seated himself firmly on target. I always distracted other kids and they watched in amazement, not knowing what was about to happen. I turned the generator handle in a quick spin, and the math's teacher watched the kid hit the roof in pain and amazement. I packed the gizmo away but was shopped by one of the girls in the class. Gizmo and I went to the office where I was caned three times and made to explain what the gizmo was and why I brought it with me. "A show and tell perhaps?"

These boring classes taught me one thing however. They were the media through which I learned to imitate and take off people. I could impersonate anyone. Soon all the teachers heard about it and I was put on stage at school to impersonate people as part of a school festival. From then on, I was the man. I was also the clown, but I was not the drug addict and I was not the violent person or shoplifter. Just a clown who made people laugh, sometimes at me, sometimes with me. It turned out to be my strongest weapon in the future, helping me make friends, raise money and diffuse tricky situations. The headmaster was unwittingly the Fagin of my life. The school was where I learned to be the Artful Dodger. I was quick on my feet and quicker in my mind. I got into trouble and learned to get out of trouble. Sadly, I got into it more of it than I was able to get out of, the early days. Later, that all changed.

Chapter 10

Toy Soldiers
Or
Mind Control

Whilst at school, I disliked extracurricular activities. Partly because cricket and tennis were too slow for me and partly because it interfered with my impulse to leave the school grounds as soon as possible, so I could go home and enjoy myself. There was another activity which really aggravated my boredom and that was Paramilitary Cadets. It was school's version of the military and in South Africa, all schools had one day a week of being a soldier. We would have to wear our military attire and after school, we would have to parade on the field, undergo inspection and then be drilled. It was amazing to see kids only a year or so our senior, given rank and then put in charge of marching us up and down the grounds. They would come and inspect us one by one, sometimes followed by a teacher. One occasion a kid whom I did karate with inspected me and began screaming because my puttieswere not white enough and the badge on my hat was not sparkling. He went mad at me and I said, "Ralph, what's wrong with you, why are you being like this?"

He replied "Extra parade, Gould!"

That one action really hurt me so badly. It hurt because I could not understand how a person I knew, once given rank would turn and scream at me, seemingly from the heart. What was so serious about this stupid badge or stained putties. A tear did collect in my eye and rolled out onto my cheek. Only one tear though. This one-minute episode made me understand more than anything how Mind Control [3] was part of governing. You could corrupt an innocent human by giving him power and turning him against his fellow humans. The military marching, the repetitive turns and commands all served to create a false reality within the crazy reality of Apartheid South Africa. People shouted; they did not talk. What was this silly game? It became so disturbing to me that I had to work a way of getting out of it, which was near impossible. A typical cadet field was made up of squads of cadets, each with Corporals, Sergeants and various commanders. The teachers would pace up and down watching over everyone. They were the supreme commanders, untouchable. Then at the end of the field was the brass band, seemingly immune from extra parade and from being screamed at. The band was something I had to infiltrate. Being tone-deaf would make it somewhat more of a challenge.

The next day I told the teachers that I had to join the band because my passion was to be a trumpeter. I did not know how to blow on one let alone play one. It just happened that on that day, they were short of a trumpeter and I got the position as if the gods in heaven were helping me. Strangely enough, I was to stand next to another trumpeter called Morris, a deaf mute with wires coming out of each ear and connected to a box on his hip.

Morris was given this position because of his handicap and was tolerated. He was deaf as a dodo but a great chap and highly intelligent. His school results were bad but that was because even with his hearing kit, he still could not catch every word. He could read lips from fifty feet away and we often asked him to do so for fun. He was huge, with legs like tree trunks. A gentle giant. I honestly thought he could play the trumpet and I asked him for lessons. He said he would demonstrate to me the 'general salute'. I watched carefully as he licked his lips, turned up the volume on his box and blew away. He played the general salute all in one key, a series of bursts, no different to Morse Code. However, the finger movements on the buttons were correct and that was really what I was after. After a few days, I was able to press the correct buttons on the trumpet; however, I was never allowed to play at home, simply because my sound was worse than Morris's. I was now a member of the cadet band and the following Thursday a Major Phillips was coming to drill the band. Major Phillips was a retired Army Major who was hired by schools to drill the men so they would be fine soldiers one day, as South Africa had a compulsory military draft. When students completed their schooling they went straight into the army to defend White South Africa against these invisible communists. Finally on the day, Major Phillips turned up, not in uniform, but did not stop screaming and swearing at us. He drilled the Bandleader, the person who holds the mace. The mace guided the whole band because the noise was just too loud to hear a command. You had to play and keep an eye on the mace, you know, you had to concentrate. That was not very easy for me. The band was set to march. The mace was parallel to the ground signaling that we just had to mark time, marching on the spot. Then the mace moved up and we were off. Major Phillips was watching and listening. It was a tune that was quite simple but the buttons on the trumpet were not familiar to me on this one. He screamed for the band to halt.

"I cannot put my finger on it but there is something wrong with the sound. You sound like a pack of constipated jackals. Why, I have an aunt on the farm back home with a cow that can fart better than this sound!" he screamed.

Nobody laughed. We were petrified. He walked up and down, eyeing each one of us. We all looked to the front. He looked at me and came right up close.

"Your trumpet is dirty, private. Where has it been man? Has it been up your back passage? You cannot come on parade with a dirty trumpet," he shouted.

Then he moved past me, to Morris. Morris was sweating and I felt for him; he was such an easy target.

"YOU!" he screamed at Morris, "You with the built in radar, can you hear anything?"

Morris was squinting sideways so he could read the Major's lips.

"Yed I tan" he said in his special beautiful impaired speech.

"Come-on then, let's get on with it," replied the Major.

By now, my mind was not on the sequences of this parade, my mind was clearly on the amount of sweat that fell from Morris's brow, the tremble of his lips when they met the trumpet, and the nervous movements when he marched. I knew this was going to be the worst day of his life and my eyes would squint from peering at Major Phillips to peering at Morris, right next to me. Nobody had realized that it was my playing that was causing the trouble. I just mimed on. We were in full march, the mace was all over the place and we followed merrily. The drums were banging, the symbols were clashing and the trumpets were noisy as ever. We were to be led by the bandleader to the front of the parade ground where the Major would address the whole squad. I could see he was furious with us and my attention once again was on the Major and Morris. Morris's attention was purely on himself, his little deaf world, making the right movements by heart and dancing the dance of our world, but alas as we got to the front of the field, the mace went up for us to halt in three steps, which Morris and I simply did not see. The band all halted in unison, but Morris and I kept marching. We were at the back and we bashed into the people in front of us. Morris, weighing twice my weight, knocked over two people. That was it, the Major had us pulled out and we were escorted to the prefect's room where we waited until after the parade for our punishment. It came after one hour. The two of us had to stay on the field for two hours, being drilled by a teacher and given a severe warning that we would have a high price to pay if we did this again.

They would never understand it, but the importance of this bunkum was not even registered on my list of things to follow. I could not see the point in being shouted at by friends, watching them turn into these mad machines. Playing toy soldiers once a week. What could be so important? This incident was just one of many that I endured whilst at school. Distraction was easy in a boring environment.

"You cannot control my mind. My rank is COSMIC ADHD and I am proud of it sir"

It is a handful of people who control nations
They create a world within a world,
an army outside of an army.
They hide in the shadows of large corporations.
They control the media so they control the mind.

I had seen the result of mind control, hurt by a friend
Society must percolate this truth outwards
and create new infra structures.
This is because these rogues will be exposed .
Star visitors at this point in time are coming
to the people as pure light, consciousness and
through the internet,
They are dancing erratically through the skies.
They are talking to some of us – they are not happy.
Download from my knowledge capsule – Neil Gould

"*In the councils of government, we must guard against the acquisition of unwarranted influence, whether sought or unsought, by the military-industrial complex. The potential for the disastrous rise of misplaced power exists and will persist*".
Eisenhower's Farewell Address to the Nation January 17, 1961

Chapter 11

Like attracts like
Or
Funny people like Jack and me

At the age of 15 and 16, I was getting thrills from riding motorcycles. Some pals were doing drugs but for me there was no point. The smell of marijuana made me anxious, LSD was a scary thought, *(luckily for me I avoided it)* but the pressure was on by the peers. The most dangerous part of life for the ADHD kid; peer pressure. Firstly, he is part outcast and secondly, he has to get attention to be liked and to feel part of the gang. Self-esteem is at its lowest. How hard it is for an ADHD kid to be coerced into taking drugs to be part of the gang? How hard is it for an ADHD kid to be forced to steal a car or shoplift in order to feel macho and gain glory? With such low self-esteem, an ADHD will do anything to be liked or to feel tall. Please read this again and pay attention. These are the kids who end up in jail, or end up killed in gangs. If they are not diagnosed early enough and treated, they fall through the net. Society has cast them out. Just as lepers and the unclean were cast out of the temple in Jerusalem by the high priests, so are our ADHD kids from society.

One thing is for sure; it takes one to know one. At the age of 16, we had moved to the area of Glenwood in Durban. A few houses above us lived a family who had a son of 22. He was a giant but a gentle giant. ADHD, paranoia, slight retardation, call it what you want but poor old Jack had it. He was the laughing stock. Whilst doing his accountancy articles he had an accident whilst trying to pass wind discreetly in the office. The quality of the audio alerted his peers as to the impending wave of odor. Poor old Jack was ushered into the bathroom whilst he removed his underwear. Without really washing them, he placed them for safety in his Tupperware lunchbox. That was Jack. He did not know how physically strong he was. As a kid, I befriended him in our karate class. His mental age was more like mine than that of an articled clerk. One punch from Jack and you had to take flying lessons. He could not gauge how hard he had struck you. However, every week he was there, training with us. One night I received a call from him. He was able to take his dad's old-fashioned car and even on a school night I was allowed to ride through town with him, attracting attention. We had great fun and great laughs. Behind it all was Jack's plan to find females. He never admitted it until one night I received a call. Jack told me he had a girl in his house and that I should come round and 'share' her with him. Well for me this was a feast. What 16 year old had it on a plate? The problem was that he had picked her up and taken her to his parent's mansion whilst they were on holiday. He was being most persistent in trying to get her into bed but she was scared of him. Jack wanted me to calm her down. I spoke to her and assured her that he was harmless, just a big kid who was horny. The sequence of events that followed I shall never forget for the rest of my life. Jack whispered in my ear that I was to take her into the next room and "do" her, but that I should wait three minutes so that he had time to get into the wardrobe. I waited, and then went into the room alone to see if he really was going to sit in the wardrobe and watch. I opened the door and there was Jack, naked and clutching a small jar of Vaseline, sitting on a precarious shoe shelf. I shut the door; gob smacked, and went to fetch the woman.

We got onto the bed and started to cuddle. She said she did not want to take off her clothes. I told her we should just romp on the bed, clothed, and she was to pretend she did not know that Jack was in the cupboard. I suspect she thought I was kidding. All of a sudden, there was a crash, the cupboard door flew open and Jack fell out, Vaseline and all. The shelf had collapsed. The young woman must have gotten a severe fright. She took off in shock and bolted out of the house. Jack put his glasses on and calmly asked me, "Where shall we go now?"

As crazy as Jack was, he too had a purpose in life. The man brought me many moments of happiness. When I was down, he picked me up. People laughed at Jack. I never did. He had a heart the size of a pumpkin. I decided a few weeks ago to track him down after all these years. He was married and still in South Africa. He had retired from a Government Customs audit post and was living a life of fear. He believed that people were trying to hunt him down for being so honest all his life. After half an hour on the telephone, I realized that poor Jack had slipped. He had other mental problems, which had overcome him. His brother had committed suicide a few months ago; evidently, a disturbed gene ran through the family.

During the summer holidays, our South African seaside town, Durban, thronged with holidaymakers. We looked forward to the arrival of the Johannesburg boys. They were richer, faster, modern and from the big City of Gold. Kids of 17 came down in E type

Jags with no licenses, given by their rich fathers. At this point, the Johannesburg boys and girls fascinated me. They were warm and full of fun. Upon meeting them, we would wade in the summer memories, recalling the fun we had in the previous summer. I had two particular friends come down each year. Both were handsome and extremely vain, constantly looking in the mirror, and combing their hair. Each had their own bottle of Neo Medril, a cortisone based cream, which they would rub into their chorbs (*teenage pimples*). Each one asking the other how he looked. I would watch in amazement; I never gave a damn how I looked. Man, I barely wore shoes until the age of 13. Comb my hair? I had a mop and a mop it stayed. As soon as Alan and Richard arrived, they called me and I came down to see them in their holiday flat on the beachfront. I came on my 50cc Yamaha motorbike. You had to be 16 to ride one and 18 if you wanted anything larger like a 250cc bike, which I had in the garage, conditional by my father that I would not touch it until I was 18. My 18th birthday was two weeks away. So far, I had been amazingly cooperative and obedient. The fear of losing it kept me away from it. It was parked in our garage at home. I was allowed to start it and drive up and down the driveway, but on the street, no way. It was illegal and the police were strict. We hugged each other when we met and immediately recalled the time when another of their friends had driven us around last summer and stopped in an apartment complex, siphoned the petrol out of someone's car and put it into theirs, and how the Zulu watchman threw his Knobkerrie at the car during the escape and broke the back window. We laughed at all the stories about the different girls we picked up; I was more the spectator because I was not as confident with the girls when the Johannesburg boys were around. Perhaps it is because I never had any Neo Medril or perhaps because my self-esteem was severely affected by my tics, which I did hear the girls snigger over on a few occasions. I wanted to bury myself.

Alan told us of his recent 18th birthday and how he had received an 180cc Yamaha. I spurted out that I had a 250cc Yamaha. Both boys laughed at me, thinking I was just trying to get one better.

"I have, honestly," I said. "Where is it then?" they scoffed. "At home," I replied.

"Well if you had one, you would ride it," said Alan.

"In Johannesburg I was riding an 180cc at 16 years old," said Richard.

The feeling of them thinking I was lying; the thought of my metallic red bike waiting for me was getting too much.

"I can show it to you if you come to my parent's house," I blurted.

The boys laughed it off and I spent the best part of the evening talking about the bike obsessively. I did not want them to think that I did not have one. It drove something in me crazy, started a buzzing, whirling engine. It grew louder and stronger and I could not overcome the urge to get it, I could not over come the urges in my head. The brain was crying for something, it felt thirsty, brought on by this teasing between us all. I knew I had two weeks to go and had been good for two months. My mouth went dry as the thought of going all the way home to get it occupied my mind. I had to go, and go I did.

I went home, turned my 50cc engine off at the driveway and sneaked it into the garage. I first pulled the 250cc out of the garage, moving quietly so as not to wake my parents or the Zulus in the Kaya. I parked the 50cc and wheeled the 250cc up the driveway and into the road. I freewheeled down the hill and a few hundred meters away, I turned the key and pressed the electric start. The red, green and orange lights lit up the speedometer. The sidelights kicked into action and the engine roared with delight. It was sitting between my legs, this awesome machine of power. The colors of the lights distracted me from the fear of what I was doing and the acceleration left my stomach somewhere behind me up the road. I was in heaven once again, I was flying, my brain had its thirst quenched at last, the wind blasted past my face and the gears sang their 5-gear melody as the Yamaha revved away. No effort at all, just pure power and speed took me over and before I knew it, I was back at the beachfront beckoning the boys to come down.

Only Alan came down and he wanted a ride on the back. I sat him behind me and played the five-gear song. He was holding on for dear life. Hands left the crash bars and wrapped around my waist. A Johannesburg boy holding me around my waist was an honor.

I revved up the main highway toward the direction of my home. Over the beautiful roar of the engine, I suddenly heard Alan screaming. Another sound joined the din, a siren. I turned around and saw the blue flashing light following us. I could not be caught. It was too late; I had broken a promise to my dad. Fear took over and I kicked the gears up and shot down a side road, zigzagging between streets. In no time at all, there were four police cars after me. I had one thing in mind and that was not Alan, it was to get away and put the bike back and go to sleep like this all never happened. Sadly, my Steve McQueen moment was cut short at the Willow Vale junction as five cars hemmed me in. The police officer pulled me off the bike whilst the black police officer held it up. Alan was thrown to the floor.

"We nearly shot you, you bastard thief" said the policeman. "I am not a thief" I replied, "It's my bike." "You bloody liar, I will fix you good, come" said the police.

They were taking me to the crime scene, the scene where this bike had been reported stolen. Three cars in front, two cars behind and the threat of deadly force if I absconded. Poor Alan was in the cage at the back of the car. He was white. I forgot about him. I forgot about the arms around my waist and how impressed he was. I wondered where this crime scene was and slowly as we headed into a familiar neighborhood, it dawned on me.

"Sir, we found the buggers", "Sir we nearly shot them, but we would have shot each other the way he was driving".

My poor dad was "Sir". My mom was looking out the window, standing next to our Zulu servant, who had heard a strange noise in the night, discovered the Yamaha was missing and called the police.

My Dad said, "I am terribly sorry, it's my son. He must have snuck in and taken the bike." How was I to get out of this? Wait, it gets worse.

In no time, my dad had about 10 cups of tea served for all the police and they relaxed and took delight in the fact that they were able to catch me, boasting about how they could have shot me. The Sergeant then asked to see my license. A month before, I had forged my 50cc license into a 250cc license. This, the police would not let go.

My mother spent the next week begging the police to let this one ride. The Dutch white Policeman tried to put my mother into a compromising situation in order to drop the charges. He told her he was a lover not a fighter. Over the week, the charges were dropped, as my mother was able to sweet-talk the police officers out of taking action. I was called down for a lecture and to hand in my forged license and take the test again which I did. For some reason, my dad let it go as well. Two weeks later, I was free as a bird and enjoying biking with my pal Des. People used to say he was a case of some sort, but this meant nothing to me. He had left home in Swaziland, a black state bordering South Africa. He came to Durban to look for work as a young man, just him, his backpack and his bike. It was said too that he suffered from depression and terrible mood swings. He had this terrible cough from smoking and one night we saw his chest when his shirt was undone. As a kid, his mother spilt boiling milk on him and he never developed pectoral muscles on one side and part of the other side. As a result, he was severely scarred and would never engage in talk with the girls. I assume he had a complex about this, but with me, someone who only saw his spirit, he was completely at home. No secrets, just honest stories about his life in Swaziland and how he felt about himself. Stories that to this day, I keep to myself. Sadly, one night on his bike, Des was killed. This was something entirely new to my reality, which I had to experience. After a bout of mood swings, Des stormed out on his bike and hit the curb at 80mph. It took his leg off. He died in the ambulance. I saw the bike that night covered in Des's blood. I could not understand what it meant. My mother told me repeatedly that Des was dead. I went to see a girlfriend of mine and she explained it to me. I was bewildered. This was fun land, what happened? That was the last time I rode a bike. I left it parked at home until I found someone to buy it. Des was gone, Des understood me, he understood that when we were riding, the wind blew past our ears and the gear changes played a particular tune that only he and I knew. We would change gears not for the torque, but for the melody, look at each other, smile and let the tears spray off from both sides of our eyes. We would sniff and pull away at the next green light, perhaps for the last time together.

"Hamba gashly (Zulu:Go slowly) Des,
Remember our Bikes, our song, forever.
I will not ride again, not without you.
I will play our song only in my mind. I promise you
One day
We will sing it together again"

Chapter 12

Dumped naked
Or
Make your own way home

At this time, when I was around 15, we moved house to a block of flats on the beachfront. This was a huge change of lifestyle for me. I guess my dog noticed it more as he was used to running around and garden. From the front balcony one could see a huge park as well as parts of the ocean. From the rear one could see the local drive in cinema and just nearby was a huge patch of vacant land. My nights were pleasant and I must admit that I slept very well. Times were good and I enjoyed the local facilities very much. I was in walking distance of the local ice rink, thereby was the local drive in cinema, and across the road was the park. It was a few minutes walk to the beach and a further five minutes walk past my friend's apartment en route to the local amusement center where we would drum up free games on the pinball machines. There was a Zulu superintendent who cared for the machines. His name was Simon and each time I arrived at the amusement center called Newton's, Simon would give me a huge smile and from behind the front of his uniform he would pull out a chain attached to which were a load of keys, each one for a different pinball machine. Simon would give me free games .He was huge and tall and he had the greatest smile that one could imagine. Many a time he would save me when one or two drunken characters entered the Newton center.

My friend Larry lived on the beachfront would walk home together with me when the center was closed at midnight. During the eight minutes' walk home we would play silly games with each other, a constant battle to win small brownie points. He would wear rubber flip-flop shoes or thongs as they were called and I would try to get behind and tread on the back so that when he stepped forward he would trip up. To get back at me he'd give me a playful slap across the back of the neck. It all ended well; I wish that everything ended that well. That night I arrived home I entered the elevator and got out on the third floor and made my way to our front door. Just before I went inside I noticed a smoky mist at the end of the hallway. It was the sort of blur that you see when you have tears in your eyes, except that mine were dry. I must admit that it gave me a bit of a fright but then I had never seen anything like this before. I started to try and rationalize it in the event that I could find a good reason for this apparition to make sense and to fit into my reality. As best as I can recall I never gave it a second thought from then on.

Once inside the apartment I closed the door and pressed the lock button that was housed in the handle and proceeded to fit the chain onto the door. From what I recall I then went to brush my teeth, went to my bedroom, got undressed and went to bed in my underpants, which we called scants, since this type of attire covered the bare minimum. I went off into a deep sleep satisfied at my night outing and remembering Simon's big smile. The thought of standing on the back of Larry's thongs made me smile as I fell asleep. During my sleep I cannot recall any particular events that took place as far as my dreams were concerned, however the very next memory I have was being dropped off outside the front door of my apartment. This is beyond all doubt; there I was wearing nothing but scants with my feet on the cold floor in a daze and staring at the front door. I felt very vulnerable and I was not fully aware of exactly what happened. I was extremely tired and a little weak but I did not hesitate to bang on the front door at 3:00am in the morning. I did so and I heard the chain unlock followed by the click of the lock button in the door handle. I saw my father's hand come around the door until the familiar pattern of his pajamas filled the space in front of me. My mother was standing behind him with her hand covering her mouth and I could see that she was quite shocked to find me outside a locked apartment.

Nobody seemed to say anything about this matter and as a matter of fact it was never discussed until a few years ago when my mother brought up the subject. As time has gone by, all the strange incidents have formed a pattern of meaning for me. However the meanings are more in the form of complex files, which are stored in my knowledge capsule and have added to the overall picture of the full experience given to me by my star visitors. One thing that I can tell you for sure is that this was done on purpose. It was to show me that the star visitors have a sense of humor. You to have to admit that the picture of my parents staring at their semi-naked son outside the front door at three in the morning when there is no human explanation for this occurrence is very funny. It seems that when the human being is faced with an inexplicable occurrence, that it is best buried, the reason being that if they had told anyone then they would look silly themselves. That is what happened.

Signed Statement to Congress (8/22/1960) -- "It is time for the truth to be brought out... Behind the scenes high-ranking Air Force officers are soberly concerned about the UFOs. But through official secrecy and ridicule, many citizens are led to believe the unknown flying objects are nonsense.... I urge immediate Congressional action to reduce the dangers from secrecy about unidentified flying objects."
Former CIA Director Vice Admiral Roscoe Hillenkoetter

How the CIA Views the UFO Phenomenon, Second Look, Vol. 1, No. 7, Washington, D.C. *(5/1979)* -- "We have, indeed, been contacted -- perhaps even visited -- by extraterrestrial beings, and the US government, in collusion with the other national powers of the Earth, is determined to keep this information from the general public."

Chapter 13

Kaapi – Garland & I loved him more than ourselves
Or
A mystical mystic, bathed in alcohol and dagga

Kaapi

As kids, Garland and I grew up together from the age of 7 years old. A life long friend and truly mainstream ADD. I can recall the afternoons after school going to Garland's place and Garland coming to my place. Here were two different characters, both ADHD but each feeding off the other. Garland had sensible, high intelligence and a good capacity for reading and understanding. I simply could not read anything without the letters taking off into the air. His vocabulary was huge and his perception into history, politics or whatever, superb. However, life is a circle of events and any weak link in the circle means it collapses. There was something in his ADHD that worried Garland, perhaps causing his hesitancy in confronting people or his lack of confidence somewhere in the loop. Perhaps it was just that he saw the fickleness of people in certain situations and could not make bankable relationships with them. Garland's mother, Pearl, was the only parent who seemed to talk to me and not at me, who made me feel normal. She could tell me what to do or explain appropriate behavior to me because her explanations always ended with, "Hey?" and a big smile, as if we were equals. She was always happy to arrange for Garland and me to play together, she always ensured that either she or Pucksy, Garland's father, came to collect or drop us off at various venues. Life at Garland's was great. The level of play was always at a higher intellectual level than with Peter. It was about talking sense and about the World War and seeing mature films. Garland was my rock and my anchor and he still is today. His ADHD has supercharged his ability to size up people, especially those social climbers. He can distinguish a genuine concern from an angled visit. Charity is always close to his heart.

So you may ask, what about the ADD? Here we go. Garland was Mr. Sensible and as time went on, there was a streak of boredom developing in him. He grew more interested in what relationships I was developing with girls and began to join in with the dangerous fun. You see, once again the thirst for excitement to feed the supercharged brain comes first. Garland and I had countless adventures in the bush, sort of Uncle Tom's cabin events; encounters with snakes, immersion into dangerous bilharzias-ridden streams, getting lost and playing in shark infested river mouths, all of which ended up us both being in trouble. What was Garland's take on it? "Lekker" (*slang for great*). There wasn't a hint of danger for us, only two brains using up neurotransmitting chemicals at a phenomenal rate, rewarding our sensory perception with a halo of delight. There are times that I reflect on the encounters we had in the jungle. We were somehow connected spiritually to Mother Earth, feeling her pulsating breast as she cared for us whilst in her domain. With us caring about her creatures, never harming them, always loving them and admiring the artwork of the forest, with the web of vines coming from the trees. The clay dripping from her gullies, which we molded into cups and ashtrays. We admired her tropical fish and her mangrove crabs were a source of amazement. This early education into the workings and wonder of nature profoundly influenced the rest of our lives. Garland and I understand more than anything the importance of preserving the mangroves, an essential Garden of Eden and life source of all Marine life. We know we have seen them, smelled them, swam in them played, with them and were part of them.

Is ADD so bad? We were aware of this eco- beauty as kids. We instinctively knew that this little world of life needed preservation. Recognition of its charm, powered by lack of dopamine to the brain, caused us to forget the boundaries and limits of our playing field and to forget that we should have been home two hours earlier and to ignore the dangers of what can happen to you in the African bush. Other kids would marvel at the stories that were imparted about Garland and me and what we were up to. Shame on them, all those stars on their school charts, medals for being good, and their authority to label us as "naughty". Maybe natural and adequate production of dopamine makes your rear end stick to your seat, never quite pushing your limits, never building templates or hooks for the important groundbreaking events in the future. Many of our school pals, who were well behaved and did well in exams, surprised us later on in life. They were not really up to where we expected they would be. We, on the other hand, were not sweeping the road or collecting garbage as predicted. When we left school, Garland worked at the scrap yard of old man Skikner, an 85-year-old Litvak (*Jewish person from Lithuania*) who would buy the wares from walk-ins off the street, harboring copper wire stolen from the railways, only later to sell it back to the railways. Garland would make way for Skikner to receive his weekly vitamin injections so that the old man would be able to service his 20-year-old secretary. Garland would watch the shop, ensuring that Ganesh, his cashier-cum-book keeper, did not hive off too much of the money into his pocket. As for me? Every Jewish parent wants his or her son to be an accountant. I was sure my final school result would not be a university pass. It was not. I had to work with a firm of auditors and go at night to a technical college to be a chartered secretary. Problem was, it took six months to explain to me the difference between a credit and a debit. It may seem easy to you folk, but for me, you put money into your account – it is a credit. However, when you send money from a company account, it is a credit. The damn credit is now a debit and the debit is now a credit?! How would I ever understand that? I could not understand at my school math's lesson that if I had minus two eggs in my left pocket, and plus two eggs in my right pocket, I had no eggs. I went home crying as a kid and put two eggs into one pocket, but never figured out how or what minus two eggs looked like. I painted two eggs red, and then tried it. In the end I got two red and two white eggs, all of which were eaten

I was sent by my folks to be articled in an accounting office, along with a pal of mine, Jonah, another ADDite. We were told to tick off about 20 pages of items from one book and match them to the entries in another book. Jonah called the number and ticked his book and I confirmed it and ticked my book. After 10 minutes, the boredom hit him first, then me. We looked out the window, then at each other and without even mentioning it; we each proceeded to tick away at 20 pages without cross checking with each other. It was faster and had more validity to us to do this because it ended our boredom and saved time. From here, it was downhill until we were caught. We lasted four days.

You have to have a degree or qualification to cheat. Be a CEO of a large corporation.
Titles are painted into your reality as being sacred.

At this point, I carried on with all sorts of things to get by. Garland went into the army; I got my military service deferred. First it was the commandos, then the infantry and so on. I just could not face it. Garland finished his military service and went to university to do law. He quit after six months. Now what? Let's celebrate, man. By this time, I was really wacko. Many friends were more so, but me, I needed those natural chemicals of fun. Evidently, so did Garland. Now there was an unstoppable partnership. We lived through some of the most death defying experiences on this planet, survived and were held in the highest of esteem. We found love where others found hate, we found loyalty where others found traitors and we found life in the face of death, under the old South African apartheid era. At the age of 18, a drifter called Nutty spent some time with me. We really clicked even though he smoked dagga *(marijuana)* and I didn't. One night he was looking to score and said we were to go behind the city of Durban into the Indian/Colored zone. To go there would be to take your life into your own hands. Dirt road, shacks, gangs in the street. Nutty told me they printed bank notes and all sorts of stuff and that I had to stay by the city limits and not follow him in. That was impossible, an ADDite to stand back and not know what's going on? Are you kidding me?

We took a drive to the zone limits. Nutty made me stay and he crossed over and rode down the road. After two minutes, it was all too much for me. I followed on foot and saw an old wooden shack. Nutty seemed to be arguing with an elderly Indian man. Five colored folk *(peoples of mixed race born during the pre-Apartheid era. Many were reclassified according to their skin color, sometimes splitting up families)* were sitting on the side of the road watching all this. It seemed an eruption was imminent. Nutty was in defense mode and the crowd was not happy. Nutty shouted, "Come, let's go, quick." My eyes caught the eyes of the old Indian. His hard face stared at me and I realized Nutty had gone and there was I with the 5 coloreds and the elderly Indian man, locked into an eye-to-eye battle. Suddenly, my brain felt like it was rebooting, my body pulsated and my heart was beating like crazy. I was in a death zone but facing something so special and so amazing. I felt as though I was watching a film. I was flying above all this. The hard face of the Indian started to melt. We were still staring. No fast moves on either side. I could have been a police officer and he could have been a killer. I saw his hands drop into a non-threatening position. They hung loose by his side. His eyes glimmered through an intense web of red veins and tears. I was fascinated by this man, this poor Indian, living in squalor, surrounded by the roughest of people. His big dirty teeth finally gave me a dull reflection of the sun and I smiled back at him. We walked towards each other and for reasons beyond this earth, we approached each other, each needing each other's warmth and instead of shaking hands, we hugged. "My name is Neil," I said. "My name is Kaapi," he replied, "Come in. Come in, Come in."

I had never been into the non-white areas of town, let alone into any Indian's house. I had been in hundreds of white people's homes, you know, you want to pee, you pee in the loo and flush the chain. Not here. Just off the wooden kitchen was a room precariously balanced on stilts, with a hole in the floor looking down six feet into a bucket? No power, only a wood burner. This was Kaapi's domain. He survived by selling 'dagga'. Always in the midst of commotion and war, but a man whose heart was that of a celestial being. An old soul who had come back to earth, to make one learn about life, about poverty, even though he taught me with one foot already in his coffin. After we had sat and talked for what seemed like hours, I had to set off home. I was bewildered by the whole experience. The belief system painted in South Africa was, "Black is bad and dangerous" and you never strayed off the path. But, my, what a wonderful detour I'd taken. I just had to go back again, this time with Garland. I called him as soon as I got home and I could hear his blood rushing, I could feel he was about to break his sacred promises to his parents, he would stray off the path, dangerously so, big time. It was the next weekend that our new adventure would begin.

> *The power of this light was a valuable lesson. It was successfully used to transform a violent moment to peace.*
> *Most important, it has been passed on.*
> *I was beginning to be aware that my life was somewhat exciting and dangerous. I thought it must be for a higher reason. Please read on.*

Chapter 14

Check my 'tumb, I live in hell but I love you
Or
Come to the white man's world, it's safe at Smuggler's Inn

I could not wait until the next weekend. Garland turned up at my house in an old black De Soto, which his granddad had given him. It was a real Hollywood mobster's car, and it certainly turned heads. I directed him to the zone and then we stopped for a while to survey the scene and discuss all the "what ifs". All our other friends were at respectable places at that moment, I am sure, but us two buggers, we were just about to cross the line, a line more dangerous than the rules and boundaries declared in our growing up neighborhood. The car edged over and onto the dirt track. There were scantily dressed kids in the road, rolling a bicycle wheel with a stick and chasing it. They had right of way in the street. It was their area.

With shanty houses on each side of the road, and colored folk (*half white and half black Africans – human leftovers from the pre-official Apartheid days of the 1940's, discarded by the government*) sitting on the edge of the road on wooden chairs, drinking and smoking. Their faces were hard and their skin wrinkled from alcohol and drug abuse. The De Soto glided past on eggshells, careful not to make too much noise and slowly stopped outside Kaapi's house. We got out and headed straight for the damaged wooden front door and I knocked. After about a minute a little Indian kid, around seven years old looked up and politely said, "Hello uncle, please wait, he is coming".

Kaapi appeared and it took him a few minutes to clear the fog from whatever was in his brain. He grabbed me, hugged me, and said, "I knew you would come". He was elated and called his wife. "Ela, my brother arrived, make tea, and make something for them". I introduced Garland and Kaapi just smiled and hugged him. He told Garland that he knew me for 10 years, not realizing that I was only eight years old 10 years ago. We were back in fantasyland, with a man who gave us unconditional trust, love and friendship. Anything was possible in our talks. They were highly spiritual, in that we spoke a load of garbage, not drawn from the channels of the ether or spirit world, but drawn from the channels of the methylated spirit bottles. The warmth we exchanged was more valuable than the words and his hugs; I can feel until this day. Most of our meetings would begin by us all sitting in the kitchen on one long plank supported by two fulcrums. Three on the bench and if any on the outside stood up, the whole bench would seesaw and the others would be tipped off. The bench became known as the trap and invariably one of us, usually Kaapi, would stand quickly, leaving us on the floor. This was fun and we did it every time we visited. Not that Kaapi could remember. It appeared as a new joke each time.

Slowly we began to meet the locals. Kaapi never allowed more than two of them into the house at once. We usually went outside to meet them. They were a real mix of races: all dumped by Apartheid into this zone, a lost world. We must have drawn a lot of attention by showing up here and more and more colored people would wait outside to see what was up with Kaapi and us. We went to the car, but the tires were slashed. The chills went up our spine as the reality of the natural borders set in. The laws of nature were churning their ruthless tides into the picture, and so it began. We managed to change one wheel and limp out at just before sunset. Kaapi begged us to come back that night and we agreed but needed someone to watch the car. He promised.

We got the wheels fixed and spent time discussing the return to the zone. It was a must. Kaapi said there would be a party that night so we turned up and they sent young Cliffy to watch the car. We walked about 100 yards to a house full of gangsters of the worst kind. Drink was everywhere and sold illegally. These were called shebeens, or illegal bars. Kaapi stood by us telling everyone how we were old friends. He never left our side. He would tell people how we all used to go the Beverly Hills hotel in Durban and about the dinner parties and speeches he used to make. Anything went, any story was accepted, reality was displaced and life was cheap. Within seconds, Cliffy's elder brother ran out the house screaming, "PARA, PARA!" A fight had erupted. Bottles were being broken and people were slashed. Friends turned on friends; the hype was infectious. Many of the elders screamed to try to stop it and after fives minutes it subsided, but with one serious casualty on the floor, bleeding through a deep, near-fatal knife wound. Garland and I went up to him and supported his head to see if there was any life in him. If we were not there, he would have been left for dead. He had a pulse and we carried him to the De Soto and rushed him to a black hospital. He arrived alive, but we never heard anything of him later. Nobody cared; he was just another number, just another body, just an ex-customer of the shebeen – perhaps with no family, which was not uncommon.

Despite this event, Kaapi urged us to come back the next day. We did. Suddenly five hooded, military type figures burst into the house. They pinned Kaapi down and pushed the family around like paper dolls. They beat up a few people outside whilst their guns were drawn. You could not see any part of their skin. One of them said in a very strong White Afrikaner accent. "Close your eyes keep your head down and after this, get out of here or we will bust you". It was the secret police. They came for a raid to keep the pressure on these folk. To intercept and check for drugs or alcohol, or more likely, to let them know which race was boss. It was a very sordid affair and it upset us even more so because it was our people coming in from our zone. On the one hand, we were traitors and on the other, these people were our friends. A friendship from the inside of us, to the inside of them. Therein lays a deep message. After the raid, a huge argument broke outside Kaapi's house. Roy John Dove, a notorious Cape Colored (*another apartheid classification*) and known psycho of the area wanted our blood. He had a huge axe and wanted to get past Kaapi to get us. Kaapi was furious and screamed at Roy John, "You cut my head off first. If they die, I die". Kaapi turned his back and offered his skull to Roy John. Then I felt her, the being who visited my room as a child. I heard a sound of wind and a smell of babies. How can I explain it to you? The knowledge of this particular instance unraveled in my mind and was presented to me. I immediately walked into the fracas, looked Roy John in the eyes, and said to him.

"Roy John, it is me, Neil, remember me? We are with you".

At any time, a strike from a Panga (*a machete for cutting sugar cane*) could have ended it for us. I felt an undercurrent of energized awareness around me, I felt this field surround all of them and I felt I could control or fine-tune the intensity of the anger.

Within ten minutes, we were all hugging each other, offering each other everything we had. It was an orgy of radiant energy. Most of these people I had been acquainted with for some time now. All had fallen through the safety net, because of neglect by the South African government.

We returned the following week to find that something had happened while we'd been gone. Kaapi's tendons in his wrist had been cut. Only his thumb moved and he was so obsessed with this thumb of his, that all the hellos and bye byes were based on him asking us to "Touch my t'umb". (*Thumb*) After a few weeks of further incidents, we knew the risks had exceeded the rewards that the chemicals in our brains were receiving. Even Garland, who was braver than I, said we should cool it. He was always my anchor and leveler. He was always more sensible. We said to Kaapi, "Please meet us at the border of the zone and we will take you into our world, less violence." He agreed, perhaps because it was a good idea at the time or perhaps he did not want to let his two white brothers down. We collected him from the zone and headed to white man's town, to a club at the Port of Durban called the 'Smugglers Inn', a haven for gays, sailors, and lost white souls. Nobody would notice an Indian walk in with two white men. Most were too drunk. Kaapi was at our table, drinking in a white area, with white people. We thought he'd be safe with us.

After an hour, Garland and I saw 'Mike the Knife' walk in. I always greeted Mike, Mike always greeted me and after that, you were safe. Mike was one of our city's poor and violent whites. Despite the Apartheid government guaranteeing white men jobs before black men, he still dragged along the bottom of society. What a depraved white-skinned human this was. One hour later when Mike was tanked up, he came over to our table and pulled Kaapi up off the chair by his neck. He pulled out a long knife to slit his belly. I hurled forward and begged Mike with everything I had. I saw the look of hate in his eyes for Kaapi, because he was Indian. I felt the energy field switch on just at the correct frequency. I felt my verbal powers of persuasion slowly chipping into Mike's psyche, I saw his hand relax and Kaapi in shock slip back down into his chair, both eyes pleading with me to take him home. We did and we did so as fast as we could, not without Kaapi receiving a punch in the guts from Mike. We never went back to Smuggler's. There was no place in our world for Kaapi and no place really, in this entire world for him, except in our hearts. There was always a place in his heart for us also, because Kaapi knew something spiritual about Garland and me. He had expressed it in his own way in very personal messages between me and him, messages which told me that he knew about previous lives, life after death and about intervening beings from another world.

I could see that there was the possibility that what I was experiencing was a microcosm of the real world. I knew hardly anything about the big world out there. We had a media truth embargo with accompanying indoctrination that the Chinese communists were on the northern borders; that blacks were dangerous and so we had to go to war with them to stop them taking over. TV was not allowed, in fact there was no TV broadcasting station in South Africa at all in the mid 1970's. Yet, I was immersed in a theatre of operations and at grass roots level where I gained firsthand experience of systematic human mind control and all the accompaniments of a truth embargo.

I will have you know that at this time when the world boycotted South

Africa over apartheid, the Russians, Chinese were drinking with the South African military across the border in Botswana whilst they purchased rough diamonds used to cut into the steel of their weaponry.

South Africa had its oil supply stopped, yet the perpetrators of the embargo sat in Botswana, handing out cash for industrial diamonds in order to drill through the hard rocks to get to the oil. (The diamond invention - Edward Jay Epstein)[4]

Communication and reprogramming of our DNA, by language, and frequencies?

"*Are telepathic transfers of mental images and concepts communication from aliens? SETI (the official search for extraterrestrial intelligence) still argues that they have not received any anomalous radio signals to suggest extraterrestrial life exists. Whether this is the truth or not, that is their official line. But perhaps extraterrestrials would find radio transmissions a very primitive way to communicate. If we listen to experiencers, they say it is more likely to happen through multi-dimensional levels of human consciousness.*

'This communication happens because everything is made up of the same matter resonating at different harmonics, so that the ETs are able to communicate with us, directing thought on subatomic levels, and so activate subconscious interaction. This is interpreted by the conscious mind as a simplified form of communication, such as symbology. Symbols are meant to communicate the nature of the macrocosm.' — T.T., experiencer (WA)."

The New Human Star Children – Mary Rodwell, 2006

DANCE TO THE SOUNDS
OF THE VIBRANT
DELL TRIO
EVERY FRIDAY & SATURDAY
8 p.m. to midnite

The OUTSPAN
A Trust House

CABARET :
NEIL GOULD
Hypnotist, Master of Mime, Fire Eater, Comedian, Ventriloquist.

A LA CARTE RESTAURANT
BUSINESSMEN ! Don't forget, we also extend a warm welcome every lunchtime ! See you soon at . . .

**TRYY
UMBILO RD., DURBAN
TELEPHONE 351561 (5 lines)

Chapter 15

Enter: The Hypnotist
Or
The Ventriloquist Who Was an Articled Clerk

The hyperactivity continued distraction after distraction and I was really becoming a pain to many. I would wake up and my nerves felt raw. I can understand how other kids would use alcohol or drugs to take the edge off it. It is not something that one can describe easily, but I believed that it was normal to wake up feeling raw, feeling raw to the bone, in pain, as each nerve fiber sparks for attention. The brain was thirsty for its vital transmitters but sadly they were not there. The brain would tell me "Go and get juice. Now", and I'd have to go and find something to stimulate it. Never mind convention, never mind what you should be doing, you must get a fix. For me, attention was a way to promote a high. I started to perform. I started to perform anywhere and everywhere and once in a restaurant I started entertaining the folk around my table. This did not go unnoticed by a chap called John Halse, a local entreponeur, who owned a disco. He thought this was a chance to promote his club He offered me a few bucks a week to DJ and do my thing. I had a ventriloquist doll and in no time I'd perfected the alphabet from

A to Z without moving my lips. I was the only 'vent' DJ in town, if not the world. It drew the crowds and then John pushed me to the next stage. Hypnotism seemed natural because he noticed I had the ability to control people around me when it came to wanting to be liked. Once again, my powers of observation came to my aid as I recalled the spiel of all the traveling hypnotists who would visit our town during the summer holidays. Before long, I was the talk of the town and appeared in town halls up and down the coast. Garland was always there in the event we needed a stooge, as sometimes the audiences were drunk.

On one occasion, we did a gig at a hotel called the Outspan. For 10 years it was only locals All of a sudden, we turn up, six new faces are on stage and magically hypnotized in a blink. They never bought it. We were chased out of the room, with John already in his truck, gunning the engine and beckoning us to run and jump on the back to make our escape. We sweated and then we laughed. What else would one expect from brains that have learned how to manipulate to survive, brains that needed juice, super premium, high-octane juice?

The bookings continued. John booked me into a hall on the south coast of Durban. The show was fine; people were easily hypnotized and sleeping all over the stage. One fellow had an epileptic fit and we very discreetly removed him from the stage as though it was part of the act. One of our stagehands gave him first aid. We kept him semi imprisoned until we thought he was ok then we sent him back to his seat. After that show, we all went to the local hotel. As usual, there were always plenty of people who wanted to meet me. You must understand that in those days in South Africa 1973, there was no television. It was simply not allowed, as the government did not want the blacks to get smart or organized. Therefore, entertainment was at a premium. Another of our traveling stagehands was a remarkable fellow called Richard Upton. He was handier than any repairperson I had ever seen or dreamed of. He could do anything. When he was 17, he was welding knee deep in water. He had a serious accident with electricity, the power blew his teeth out, and I understood that he was sterile because of this tragedy. However, he was also double-jointed and his arms: body ratio was such that the arms were very strong and long and the body short. He could climb up any wall and just drag the old body along. It was amazing to see. That night in the hotel, he decided to climb up the inside of the chimney. Now I ask you, is that normal? He just went up the chimney of the hotel. We were all sitting around the fireplace and people kept coming up to ask me all sorts of questions. After a while, we had forgotten that Richard had gone for a vertical stroll.

A young woman with her giant of a hubby came and asked if anyone could be hypnotized. I said more or less and she asked if I would give it a go. I did and in a few minutes, she was out cold. I started asking questions and it led to answers, which started to embarrass and anger her husband. Before long, she was crying and he threatened to hit me if I did not stop. Many of the onlookers faded away in fear. You see, in South Africa it was very violent and anything could happen. A gun, broken bottle or a stick could have whacked me across the head. Once again, I seemed to be able to control this chap and he backed off. With some relief, I smiled, thinking the situation was over. Seeing the smile, he assumed I was laughing at him and he started to shout and move towards me. I was a good foot shorter than him and half the width. Miraculously, Richard chose that moment to reappear and he slid down the chimney, along with all the soot. The giant took one look and I could see in his face that he thought it was some kind of spook, because he said in Afrikaans, "Juslyk a spook" and he ran off fast. This goes to show the mentality of the rednecks in our part of the woods. He was already disturbed by the way his wife had been put to sleep, and my control over her. Then a black genie descends from the chimney in a puff of black smoke; that was just too much for him. The genie had long arms and a short body and white dentures, which were half hanging out. I think I was more amazed. Richard and I had some unbelievable times together, but this took the cake.

I enjoyed the short-lived fame and being the center of attention. All of a sudden from a broken down old soul, here I was, beginning to use my condition to help myself and creating my own environment. The talent was getting sharper and sharper because I'd found something I was interested in. The more I performed, the more they cheered and then more people wanted me at their parties and functions and the more bookings we had. John was collecting the cash at the gates using the Red Cross, who did our ticket sales.

Garland was a key in almost every event. He was a reserve stooge for my pickpocket act or even a stooge for a hypnotized person who had to do certain planned events. The point was that we had our own show on our doorstep. Being of high profile, I was also the target of some people who liked to take a punch at anyone who stood out. I was attacked with weapons, sometimes managing to defend my self and sometimes not. I guess I was irritating people. I mean here is this young 18 year old, not particularly good looking, twitching, acting the hero and always with pretty chicks. One night Garland and I went to the University Annual ball. Now nobody needed to worry about being attacked here. All was great until a bunch of poor white trash arrived. Mike the Knife–type people and guess whom they tried to start with. Quick thinking by Garland would prove to be the biggest trick ever pulled off in front of an audience. The Black zone was 100 yards from the University. Garland took the De Soto and went to Kaapi, who was dead drunk. Unable to raise him, Garland instead filled the car with seven of the most fearsome colored hoodlums. They were all shaved and scarred and had Pangas. They heard that I was under siege and could not wait to go into a white event and kick up hell with the support of whites like me and Garland.

By this time the white trash were still trying to get to me in the center of the hall. I was dodging them and others were trying to talk them out of causing a fracas. Not a moment too soon, the door burst open and the light was thrown on seven Panga-wielding maniacs, who charged these pieces of trash. The look on their faces should be immortalized in a picture on the space shuttle. They '*cucked*' themselves and had to get the hell away in fear of their lives. Our people were always in a state of drunkenness. We managed to hold them back and we rewarded them with as many beers as they could drink or put in the car. About an hour later, they forgot the whole event and we dropped them off outside Kaapi's at 2.00am and left. Garland and I looked at each other and I said, "Give me your t'umb". We'd survived, yet again. My knowledge capsule gave me the ability to control my environment to suit my predicament. Garland was also aware of this technique and was able to foresee many events and keep us out of trouble. We knew the nature of people. We knew people at their worst, but we also knew people at their best and we were able to live in both worlds, comfortably. Apartheid was there and we were fearful to an extent, but our stealth was far superior to that of anyone trying to track us down. The police did a huge raid in the black zone and we heard that a few of our brothers were badly beaten and had their huts demolished. Three lads were locked in the police station and had been beaten. Here is a rumor for you; would it not be just great if it were true? Two days later, two men with their faces covered threw smoke bombs into the back of the local police station. The resulting smoke caused everyone to evacuate the office area. A full box of mole bombs was used, circa 14 sticks. It led to a certain Sgt Smith and his team of legal henchmen running out the front of the station, hands over their mouths, vomiting and choking. Miraculously, two of our brothers were not in their cells and were in the 'debriefing' rooms (*blacks were only ever 'debriefed' with brute force*). They managed to escape at the same time the police ran out. The third lad did not and was still in the cell, yet free of any smoke. Damage to two police vehicles took place. We heard that the Sergeant had said that this raid was brilliantly planned. I wonder who was behind it. Say no more on this one.

This period of time was one of the most important. My knowledge capsule was guiding me through important lessons of life. Understanding gang war, secret police, mind control, evil and greed, not to mention the awful predicament of others. The satisfaction of helping others was of real value. I carry this feeling today. I can see through the cracks because I can discern the slant given by the media and religious leaders, all due to my personal experience within my South African microcosm. If the news story fits then it's true, if not then it's a lie perpetrated by institutions that stand to benefit.

Garland [right.] and Neil 1973.

Chapter 16

Africa Adieu– I miss you, you are in my bones
Or
Pendennis Castle to the UK
Or
What the hell am I doing here, in this dump?

Two months later, my dad turned on the radio. The Apartheid government controlled all the news, and whilst we had lived with this for some time, my father obviously decided that enough was enough. My dad lost his cool, switched off the radio and said, "We are leaving. Keep it quiet". In reality, I did not have a clue as to what he was talking about. I could not understand 'politics', it was something that was never discussed and well left alone. I did not understand world politics either. It was so boring and did nothing to ignite my supercharged brain. Politics, shmolitics, no, not for me. Having said that, I had a natural affinity with the black people. You see in my mind the two things were separate. The laws of Apartheid and the black people themselves. I never really understood the written word, 'apartheid'. All I know is that in my mind I have the most beautiful memories of Zulus, their warmth and their rhythm but I have sad memories of their suffering, and despite this I still could not connect their issues with the word "apartheid".

Thinking back in time as a kid, I used to be fascinated by the little picannins *(affectionate term for black pre-pubescent kids)* in the Kayas at the back of the house. It was like visiting fairies in fairyland. When everyone was out, I would stray around the back and you would always see them peeping at you, from either behind a tree or wall. They were always there. We must have been fascinating to them and at the same time they must have feared the white man, just by virtue of the trouble their parents got into by the random police raids, which resulted in beatings and sending people back to their homelands. After the little white eyes caught your attention, the black faces would break into a smiling whitewash of perfect teeth. The warmth would cut through you right to your heart and slowly they would appear in full. They would materialize out of their camouflage. They would be constantly looking around for fear of being seen by their parents or by mine. My parents would never stop this kind of interaction, but others were not quite so kind. These encounters always resulted in letting them use my bicycle or try my roller skates or even taste a piece of candy. Through this kind of play, you would learn the language, clicking sounds and all. At night, their parents would bath and feed us and they would sing the Zulu lullabies to put the white children to sleep. I cannot however forget the faces of the black kids watching the whites enjoying themselves on the 'whites only' fun fair, which traveled to our city once a year. Thinking back, it was so disgusting. Not any less disgusting was watching the picannins standing by the dustbins outside a well-known beachfront restaurant, called the Cuban Hat, eating the entire throwaways from the rich whites. The more I think about it, the more I know that I have been on a special journey of light. I feel that my visitation that night by the robed being was connected to this learning process, because I feel her, each time I encounter emotionally tough spots in my life. You see, since that visit, over time I have seen feelings of hate or jealousy leave me and those negative feelings all replaced by compassion. I cannot help but tell you that no matter what happens to me in the future, I really feel that I am special and here with a purpose. I am not throwing the old religion at you because I am not a nose puller. This is my saying for those who preach religious doctrine to people, under the shadow of 'fear of judgment'. I read in a book by a very important military scientist who became a whistleblower, Dr Michael Wolf, a comment that read, "*Life is painful; anyone telling you something different is selling you something*". How true that is. I note that the essence of ADD is to break the barriers and push them past the social limit, why? Because we damn well can, and we give you all much more room to maneuver instead of bumping against the pulpit all the time. I attribute my sense of humor to ADD and the quick way my brain works; as I've shown it has got me out of a lot of sticky situations, but has also been responsible for some awkward misunderstandings with people thinking I was trying to be smart. For example, one of my first real jobs was door-to-door selling of clothes by catalogue. The company was Richard Eberhardt. I recall one man scolding me on my return visit, which was two days before payday. He said to me, "Do not ever come back here again. Your stuff is rubbish".

"Why?" I asked, "What happened"?

He replied that he'd put the shirt I sold him in the wash and one sleeve came off. "What am I to do now?" he screamed.

My answer was, "Pull the other sleeve off, then you will have a new waistcoat"

The point being, I was serious and not trying to be funny. That is how my brain saw it. The more they said "No", the stronger I came back. The harder it was to get into offices, the more I went into offices. What a grounding I had with this company; cold calling served to increase my tenacity and sales skills, and I learned my way around the word

> *By some miracle, I bumped into my sales manager after 30 years, my teacher*
> *of cold calling. He came to a meeting in my office in Hong Kong. He was as shocked as I was to see each other. I reminded him of his habit of sucking a paperclip*
> *during sales meetings, which he would pull from a small container on the desk.*
> *I also informed him of the bad habit of the national sales manager who would clean his ears with the same paperclips and return them to the very*
> *same box. Such were my powers of observation.*

Finally, I had to break the news to Garland that I was leaving for the UK. I could see he was not a happy boy, but then neither was I. We sat on the point, a jutting jetty leading into the harbor and talked for hours staring at the view of the beachfront of Durban. I was in two minds, go or stay. The 'go', won and sadly, I was in ready mode. Within three weeks, Garland and I hugged each other and I was to leave for England. My parents flew and I decided to go on the *Pendennis Castle*, a liner that went from Durban to Southampton, England. I did not really understand, even at age 19, exactly what the implications of this move were. There I was, just scraped through school, no qualifications except my big mouth, a big fish in a small pond and I was off to the center of the world. To me, I was off to somewhere called London, where the actor Michael Caine lived. I boarded the ship and noticed a nice woman wearing a Star of David. I thought I would engage her on board and try to get to know her. Being a little hesitant, I had a bright idea. On the second night, I went to the entertainment area where there were dancing and talent shows. An Englishman was playing the organ. His name was Jack, and I will never forget him. He would play along and every time he saw someone walk across the floor or a man who was slightly feminine, no matter how when or where, he would interrupt his song and shout, "Fruit!" Of course, most people would not notice this, but being ADD, I did and it entertained me no end. I am sure it was a case of Tourettes syndrome on his part. Soon I began negotiating my way into putting on a show. The purser met with me and Jack told him that he had seen me perform in a top venue. Jack was lying. The following night, I was billed as The Great Neil, who had just come back from a tour of South America, England, USA and Canada. That was nerve wracking but what the hell, the chick with the Star of David was on board and this was my method of getting to meet her. The show went down very well and I was Mr. Famous for the duration of the voyage. You note I am not telling you much about the chick with the Star of David, the reason being that after my performance, there were so many girls after me on that voyage that I needed jump leads from Jack to be able to recharge my organ.

The ship arrived at Southampton and cold April weather hit my face. What am I doing here? My dad collected me and drove all the way to London. The sickest drive of my life. Mary Poppins was a documentary; the houses were all stuck together. The air was cold, wet, and the light quality, a disaster. I suffered many years of gloom and could not understand the reason for ending up in this prison of a place. I was to learn later the reason and it was a good one. Months of loneliness went by, my spirit broken. I could not fit in. I was too wild. My jokes were not funny and I just could not compete with acts that were free every night on TV. I saw TV for the first time and could not stop admiring it. What an invention. I was living in a backward country before. I now had to work. I ended up working in all sorts of jobs, starting right at the bottom. From ticking and checking bingo sheets at Mecca bookmaker's to working in warehouses.

Suddenly, unexpectedly, Garland called. My heart raced; he had some news for me. He was coming to London to study at the London College of Fashion. I was elated. I could not wait the months, and decided to get a better job. I ended up with one at Aquascutum, as a salesperson. The person who wrote the TV series, *"Are You Being Served?"* must have had the same job, because the incidents and the people were 100% identical.

All of the staff were gay, the floorwalker was not. He really liked me because he was a rugby fanatic and I was South African. He would always walk past and if the others were not looking, he'd fake throw a ball to me. I would pass the invisible ball back to him, and he would do a little hop skip and jump and put the ball on the try line. Once, he was caught doing this by one of the gay salespeople. To see his face change and see him regain his position and stature was amazing. The sort of, "Cough...ahem" job.

On my fourth day, the staff all seemed to run in panic to the door. "What's up?" I asked the floorwalker. Passing the ball to me carefully and slowly, he said, "Sir Charles is coming." Everyone lined up, just like on the football field and Sir Charles, who could not straighten his knees through old age, came out of this Rolls-Royce and walked though the middle of the row we made for him. Did not look left nor right, but directly at the elevator. The staff clapped and I watched this decrepit man with fat lips, Bowler hat and striped trousers as he walked with bent knees and a walking stick into the lift. He was probably thinking, "You bunch of serfs". But then again, maybe not. This was a ritual.

After a month I was bored stiff. I had passed the floorwalker hundreds of balls and he caught every one of them. I had let him score hundreds of tries and kept him amused. However, there was old Armstrong, a big tough salesperson in my department. He was bored too. He was macho gay, as I found out whilst trying to stack some shirts into the pigeonholes at the back. He sneaked up on me, jamming me in between the rows of shelves containing the pigeonholes. He told me that he would like to hang me by the gonads on the light fittings. All this time he was pressing against me with something that felt like a pogo stick. I managed to tear my way free. Aside from this slightly disturbing experience, he was actually a very friendly person, perhaps a little larger than life.

The monotony was getting to me, so I decided to use my normal method of entertaining myself. Every day Japanese tourists would come in. They could not speak English and they always spent hours looking at ties and scarves, but never bought anything. Their appearance to me was very funny, being fresh out of South Africa. Buckteeth, thick glasses and funny faces when they were looking at the ties. Normally one would approach them and say, "Can I help you sir?" They would back off and put the item down. I said to Armstrong, "Watch this." I went up to the Japanese guy who had a scarf in his hand and said, "Can I scratch your fat ass, sir? He muttered, not understanding me one bit and put the item down. Armstrong thought this was great. I now had him under my control. We could pass the time with funny events. The next Japanese man came by, picked up a tie and Armstrong approached. "Can I stick my bottom into your face sir? The Japanese gentleman swallowed, turned around and in an extremely British accent, said, "I beg your pardon, and just who do you think you are?" Armstrong went white. He could not see me. I was behind the pigeonholes crying my eyes out, laughing so loud, and just wishing Garland could have seen this one.

I had cause after nearly 30 years, to go back to London.
I decided to visit the Aquascutum store. It had changed.
I approached a young Asian sales lady, standing in the very spot where I used to. I told her how the late Sir Charles would walk in, looking straight ahead and head for the lift. I pointed to it, but it was gone, no more elevator, she thought I was nuts.
There is an example of the fourth dimension of time.
One minute it is there and the next it is not.

Entertaining aboard the Pendennis castle 1974

Meeting the captain of the Pendennis Castle 1974

Chapter 17

My jobs
or
The Egyptian With A Hole In His Shirt
or
Climbing the corporate ladder - Jew Boy

My most memorable moments at Aquascutum were seeing, in person, stars such as Ronny Corbett, Tommy Cooper, Lulu, Cary Grant, and my favorite, Kenneth Williams in the store and noticing how off-white some of them were in real life. On a few occasions, during this period I had experienced a few more of thesensations ofwaking up and being unable to move. I felt as though I had just returned or gone somewhere. It was very hard to understand because there was no meaning attached as yet.

Well, Garland had arrived and it was party time. Between his busy studies, at night we would go out onto the town. It started slowly; drunken nights for two non-drinkers trying to gain a foothold in London. One night Garland was drunk as a skunk and we nearly knocked over a policeman. Garland had the audacity, after a few bottles, to shout at the policeman and tell him to get out of the way.

I ended up giving him my t'umb between the bars of the "chooky" (*Police station*). A kind doctor doctored his blood test, and a month later, Garland got off. Drinking, or trying to drink, those days were over. We chased the girls and went to parties. We had the time of our lives, despite being put off by London itself. Garland was finished with college and had to get a job. By some fluke, we ended up in a flat together, in Maida Vale, London. When the lease ran out the flat should have been returned to the Landlord, but because we lived there, there were many illogical rules in our favor. One of which was you could legally squat – rent-free.

Later, we met old Dwekky and invited him to the squat. He was a criminal lawyer but did legal aid and was paid hardly anything for it. ADD as they come, he had a big heart and was a staunch communist. We did not like that word. We knew about it in South Africa. A communist was someone who was picked up at night by the police and never seen again. Here was a real live one, living with us, but he was fine. He was quick to eat our food, but not so quick to share his toilet paper. Born in the Sudan and carted off to a UK boarding school, he got into law. His hair was like a bush and he was as hairy as an ape. He'd never had so much fun as when he was with us. His life changed, so did ours. We had to put his shoes outside the window ledge, telling him it was so they would not be stolen. The real reason was that they stunk to high hell. Dwekky kept the Landlord off our back and he kept all the demands for bills out of our domain. One day he met a beautiful girl and left to live with her in America. She was way above his league but Dwekky was crazy about her. Three months later, he was back. "What happened?" I asked. He answered, "She left me for another woman".

This solicitor, Dwekky, who would give up his time to defend needy criminals on the legal aide system, made me realize later that he had a huge social conscience. He gave up wealth to help kids in trouble. It took me many years to think about this because at the time, we thought our buddy was just a nutcase communist. In fact he was a very caring man and it is sad that in those early days of my later twenties, ADHD was not in anyone's vocabulary. This concept of a caring man should have been obvious to me but I never realized it, a clear result of Apartheid brainwashing. He was a Socialist, a caring one at that. We had terrible arguments between us, all political and all about wealth creation. Some of what he said then, I agree with today but not in the same revolutionary terms that he spoke about. That was just his immaturity at the time. We decided to go to America for a holiday together. He swore he would leave his boots outside the door if I went along. As usual we were on the prowl for adventure and women. Dwekky told us he had a friend in San Francisco who'd be away for a week, the house would be empty, and we could stay there. He did not have the address but said he remembered it so well because of all the letters he used to write. We were lucky in that some South Africans from LA lent us their VW car. We drove to Frisco with Dwekky singing all the old songs from Woodstock, telling me he wanted to show me Haight-Ashbury. He was about seven years our senior, and loved the 60's hippy era. We got to a road and Dwekky said that he thought this was the place. We drove down two other roads to be sure but he was reasonably convinced that we had arrived at the correct address. This was confirmed by the fact that the key was under a flowerpot. We went in, went to the fridge and ate most of what was left by his friends. The layout of this American house was strange to us, and the bathroom only had a curtain for a door. Nevertheless, there was a bed for Dwekky and myself and we sank gratefully into it, exhausted from the drive.

At two in the morning a girl came in and said, "Hey are you Ross's friends?" Dwekky replied that we were Bernie's friends. She didn't know Bernie, but said that Ross was her boyfriend and that any friend of his was a friend to her. Obviously the word 'friend' had different connotations stateside, as we were shortly to find out. She got into bed with us and started to pant. "Hit me" she said. Our socialist solicitor spent his time campaigning *against* violence, but this was no deterrent. She pulled Dwekky on top of her and it was only five seconds before I was a spectator in the front row of a sex show. "Hit me you bastard", she said to him. Dwekky was nervous and giggly at the same time. "Where should I hit you?"

"On my tits you idiot, smack them, harder, harder". Dwekkys' gentle touch was no match for her. My sharp brain realized that we were in bed with a maniac in America and I was now convinced that we were not in the house that we should have been. I told him to keep her busy whilst I packed the car and got it ready. I signaled Dwekky with two beeps of the hooter and he ran out, naked, with his underwear in his hands and we escaped. We headed south as fast as possible and found a motel along the Big Sur Highway. We were exhausted and waited till the morning before we had a good think about what might have happened. That experience was nothing to what happened next.

We got up late the next morning and drove towards LA, roof down as we filled with gas. A beautiful girl was hitch hiking just outside the gas station. Of course, we could not let the opportunity pass. ADD folk know that they must satisfy curiosity or let's say ADD people cannot avoid curiosity. Brain chemicals buzzing, we stopped and she got in.

"Where are you heading?" I asked. She replied, "LA", and I said that we were heading that way ourselves. She asked where I was from, and when I said England, she said,

"Gee I love your accent", a common response in America. After the banter, Dwekky switched on the radio and we caught the tail end of the news. An attractive 25-year-old had escaped from a mental hospital and was dangerous. People were advised to report her and not to approach her. My sphincter was pulsating so hard that it must have been chewing a hole in my underwear. Dwekky had that face, the face when he does not like a situation. The face that says, "MAN we are in serious trouble again. Why are we always in trouble?"

"Shall we stop here and have a bite?" said Dwekky, his tone solemn and not chirpy as before. This signaled fear; even I felt it. She turned around and said, "You're trying to throw me out, RIGHT?"

I stepped in and assured her we were not. We stopped the car and parked parallel to the pavement outside the takeaway. Luck stepped in; the girl wanted to make a call. I assured her we would wait and Dwekky gave her ten dollars, another reflex of fear. I snatched it back and gave her loose change. She was ten feet from us, dialing a number on the telephone. I started the car and put my foot down. I did not turn back, I did not want to know anything, I just wanted to get the hell out of there and head to LA. It seemed whenever Dwekky and I were out on holiday trouble followed us, or was it us who found the trouble?

Well, it was back to London, the squat, back to all the parties and time for me to lift my standards and get a better job. I had suffered so much coming this far. There were some great moments but I had to really lift myself into the real world that is if I planned to get married one day or planned to have holidays and all the things people want. I answered an advert for sales rep for a food wholesaler. I went along to the appointment, the manager called me into the room and his secretary brought me to the chair right in front of his desk. He proceeded to ask me questions, never looking up once. The secretary came in and placed a mug of coffee on the desk. How nice, I started to drink it. Suddenly I saw he too took a drink from the same cup. Obviously, he never saw me take my sip. It was his coffee, not mine. With that in mind, I was a little shaken. After the interview, he got up and was still talking. He seemed to stare curiously at me as though I was some sort of two-headed monster. He walked towards me and I walked out the room, backwards, as a sign of respect. I sort of remembered where the door was and just listened to him talking about what he expected from a candidate. I felt the door handle behind me and opened it, still facing him and stepped backwards when I suddenly felt a jab in my back. I had backed into a fitted wardrobe. I pulled myself together and understood just why this person had been staring at me the whole time. He was what I call 'Oil'; the ADD folk are called 'Water'. He just did not understand me, then I suppose, who would have?

No, I did not get the job. Stop asking. I went for another interview, this time it was in a basement flat. The interviewer was absolute 'Water', a professional recruiter. He was recruiting for Imperial Tobacco, Rothmans. He did the whole show, like "What makes you tick?" and "What if…" and, "Supposing that…" He offered me a cigarette and I said, "Sorry, I do not smoke." He looked at me as if I was mad. "You don't smoke? Why the hell should I employ you then?" My answer was spontaneous. I had learned to dance on my feet at Richard Eberhardt, remembering the sleeve that fell off the shirt.

I replied, "Sir, my brother works for Tampax but he doesn't use them."

His reply was, "You got the job and I will be very happy to have you on board. This is the first time in history we've taken on someone who doesn't smoke."

This was a real few rungs up the ladder for me. A real job with a car, expense account and training. My brief was to meet up at the Rothmans training facility, a stately home in the country where all new recruits are put through training and taught how to overcome objectives. The very first thing that happened was we were shown our rooms. Then we all went for dinner and met in the lounge to chat. There were about 30 of us.

The next day opened with an indoctrination ceremony. A Sergeant Major-type character, stern and tough, asked each of us what brand we smoked. I said nothing and he seemed to ignore it. However, anyone who pulled out a pack of the competitor's brand had him jumping on the box of cigs and destroying them. He then made the person swear at the box and tell everyone how much he or she hated that brand. He soon reduced all these people into babbling baboons, so serious, so committed so controlled. After that spiel we started doing the closed circuit TV presentations. A trainer would act as the shop customer and I would walk in, ask if I can merchandise their shelves, and put our point of sale stickers up on the gantry. Then there were various handshakes and overcoming objection techniques. A camera on me? Boy, an audience. Well, I would do my own spiel. I would walk in and miss his hand or I would ventriloquise a cat in my bag. I actually was able to coax the trainers into playing along and getting a laugh or two. It obviously motivated everyone and raised interest in the sessions.

That night, two men, part of the team came up to me. In a very serious tone, one said to me, "You are very aware," as abruptly as that. The other said, "You are, are you not?" I said, "Yes, but about what?" They walked off without another word, and I never saw them again. This has always stuck in my mind. They were there, but nobody recalled their description when I spoke about this event later.

Anyway, I had got through the training and was awarded my new car. My Granddad made it to the UK and I thought I would tell him the registration number, as I knew any toilet talk would liven him up. The car registration number was POO 1. I drove off in my POO 1 vehicle and headed for the squat. The car was filled with samples. My job was to be a relief rep. That meant standing in for reps that were on holiday or sick, so I learned my way around the UK in no time and I learned a lot in the process. Namely, that everyone had his or her own scam. Many reps never visited the calls they claimed to have made. I was not going to get into trouble for this and had to at times hint that I had gone, but the call cards were not matching. My boss loved this. He loved that fact that I was able to get on with anyone and everyone. I had one problem. I could close deals, but I had no killer instinct; I could not hurt a fly or cheat. All the reps sold their samples, but whenever I arrived at a small shop and the occupants were obviously struggling, like an old couple, I gave them the samples for free. It made me feel so good when they smiled and were happy. There was another old Indian couple that never closed their shop that I gave free samples to, in exchange for tea or a sandwich.

At the Annual dinner, I was asked to pass the salt by some very disgruntled rep. I had been on his patch and the area manager had uncovered the scams. I had not reported anything. The guy said to me "Hey, Jew Boy, pass the salt." I said, "OK, here". With my magical dexterous hands, I was able to unscrew the top of the saltcellar in one movement whilst passing the salt. As he poured the salt, the lid and all the contents of the saltcellar fell into his soup. "There," I said, "The Jew boy delivered a miracle for you."

He held his ground, whilst everyone laughed at him. This was not a bad guy, just ignorant and in time he would probably learn. I soon realized that I was amongst a certain level of people, some of who were just up to the maximum of their capabilities. Most of them were nice but I had to move on. I handed in my resignation and the Divisional Manager called me into his office. It was the first week of July and he said, "This is for you. Happy Birthday," and gave me a bottle of champagne. This knocked my socks off and I was a little emotional. Why would he do this? He was a top brass and never lowered himself. He said, "I knew we would not be able to keep you too long and I wish you luck"

I went back to the squat and wanted to try to work for myself. I had met an Egyptian, Samir Mustapha. A very smart, cultured man of my age. He said I could make money because he could bring the Arabs and I could get the goods. It all sounded simple.

Our first encounter was with a man called Mohammed Ishmael. All I had to do was accompany him and Samir to various shops and he would buy retail, pack a case and take the cases to Cairo. We got commission from the shops and commission from Mohammed. The following trip, Mohammed asked that I take a suitcase to Cairo, he would pay my fare and I would deliver the case to his cousin, also named Mohammed Ishmael. He was to be located at a hotel in Cairo and would be in the lounge at 2.00pm. I walked into the lounge and shouted out, "Is a Mr. Mohammed Ishmael here?" More than seven people stood up. One of who said, "Ah, Mohammed sent you from London, welcome." Here I was, a Jewish person in Egypt, after a war with Israel, staying with a Muslim family. I was taken into their homes, I was taken out to restaurants, I was spoiled rotten and I was accepted as a family member. I was treated with respect and kindness. My needs were fully taken care of; I was breaking the traditional mould of keeping clear from your enemy. The people themselves had nothing against Jews personally; only the politicians inflamed the fire. These religious differences were never brought up in front of me. Not because of business, but because these people were good people, and they would have truly washed my feet had I arrived out of the desert and into their tent.

I returned back to London to meet Samir and to share the cash payment. We were happy.

Samir had a big Yorkshire buyer of cotton material come into town but his Egyptian supplier had left already and Samir had lost his sample. We had only an hour to decide what to do. Samir was dressed in his grey pants, white shirt and blazer. I had an idea. I got a pair of scissors and cut a huge hole in the back of his shirt. I now stapled the cotton patch onto a card so it looked like an official sample. Samir thought I was mad, and he got even madder because nobody showed up and he had just lost a good shirt.

I would say that the Arabs were the most interesting and charming of all the people we dealt with. They certainly knew how to cut a deal but more so, how to extend courtesy and make you feel good. At the end of my relationship with Samir, I decided to go to Egypt to explore the pyramids as well as all the upper Egyptian sites. This was to be an interlude before I would take another step up the ladder into the world of civilized business. I landed in Cairo and joined a pre-organized tour of about 12 people. We met our English tour leader at the airport and were carted off to a hotel. The food was great and we planned the next step, which was to sail up the Nile on three feluccas (*old Egyptian wooden sail boats*). There were about four guys and eight girls. We did a tour of the pyramids the next day and the following night, a sound and light show from a vantage point where we could see an enormous amount of ruins. An eerie feeling came over me, whilst I imagined life on those days. Were there really gods from the stars running the place? Was the civilization very advanced? It was hard to tell as nothing supernatural came through to me, just an appreciation of a possible advanced civilization, which had been influenced perhaps by ETs. I did struggle to understand how on earth they built these pyramids. When you stand next to them, the stones are damn huge. I was more foxed when someone said that there is good reason (*and I did not see any good reason*) to assume that the pyramids were built from the top downwards, using antigravity. However, the visit was a definite anchor point for my fast evolving mind, which much later on led me into reading many theories of ET involvement in the pyramids. Strangely, over the years I began to read and watch many lectures by Richard Hoagland, a physicist and former NASA consultant, adviser to Walter Cronkite and CBS news. It was the 'Face on Mars' and the 'tetrahedral physics' that caught my attention and imagination.

We boarded our feluccas and learned to take water from the fastest flowing part of the river, which was the center, and to add chlorine tablets. At night we slept under the stars. Our captain was straight out of the bible. His name was Amoun. At times we got very sunburned and at other times we just flaked out from the heat. There were many palaces and strange ruins along the banks of the Nile all the way up to Aswan. We visited the Abu Simbel temple and stood in amazement at the view. Coming back to Cairo we boarded an old colonial train, with very fancy dining cart, along with all the old British cutlery and plates. I teamed up with a lovely Dutch girl and we shared a cabin all the way back to Cairo.

Now it was back to reality, the squat was great and we had a new lodger, an Italian, who was the gigolo of North London. A different girl every night and it was hard to sleep with all the screaming. He would hammer away all night with them and upon completion would sneak into our joint cupboard and take a toilet roll. We had strict laws on the toilet rolls. Each person had to buy his or her own. Vincenzo would never buy any.

One day Garland's dad came to visit us and as we walked in together, Vincenzo bolted out of the toilet, white as a sheet and placed his rear end into the sink. Reason? We hid the toilet rolls. I had to raise myself above all this; it was time to get a proper job from which I could benefit. However, I had a basic matric, no A-levels, therefore no university. Commodity trading took my fancy. I decided to look for a position and there was an interview, which required A-levels. Off I went into the city of London. I arrived at the company and was told to wait, as I had come early. Each time the door opened a candidate left and I got a glimpse of my interrogator. A clean-shaven man, perhaps 58 years old, with silver hair, glasses and a dark suit. I felt way below my class, never mind my qualifications. I was getting rather nervous and almost decided to leave. What had happened to my mind and those powers of control?

"Mr. Gould, please go through," said a female voice that later became known to me as Angie. I went in and the gentleman extended his hand and said, "My name is Tom Barnes. How are you?" I answered that I was fine thanks, and he took some interest in the fact that I was talking with a South African accent. I mentioned my Granddad was from the North of England, Leeds in fact, and he stared at me and slowly his face cracked and he almost melted in his chair. We spoke and spoke for what seemed like hours, and in no time we got onto the subject of toilet jokes and I let him have it. He was gasping for air and crying with laughter. I said, "What about the other candidates outside?" He looked at me and said, "Sod them, make sure you are here early tomorrow." I got the job and not only that, it was 7,500 pound per year, more than Dwekky earned. He was on 5000 pounds. Tom sent me to night school to learn about Maritime law. I learned about arbitration and how the markets work. Tom was rewarded because I started up a whole new aspect of selling. The commodities were all different types of nut kernels, shelled or in shell. We did the physical and futures market, but my brain could never understand futures. It was not natural to me; I preferred to sell off all the physical stocks in the event a futures contract was never sold. Upstairs was the date and dried fruit department and the director in charge tasted every sample that he received. Tom would often scold him for leaving a very messy 'khazi' as he called it. I learned much from Tom and I could see that secretly he was a renegade himself. He was stricken with alcoholism, MS and a few other complaints, but he certainly looked after me. He said to me, "Neil, I have no worries about you. You will be fine in the future."

Boy, do I miss this man Tom
He peered into another place from time to time
He had the edge, he gave some to me

I could look back now and see exactly how this mission to the UK was reshaping me, how it was bringing in a sense of proportion, how I started to understand responsibility, law, the seriousness of making an offer of goods for sale and of course collecting the money. At this point I felt that time was moving on and my brain was struggling to focus at times. It needed more stimulation, a hell of a lot more stimulation. It needed to take more risk, more challenge, which is strange as most people would be happy to be settled. I was not and it is not explainable. I had gained somewhat more credibility with people but not enough. Again, time to move on. I briefly passed through an impossible job working for a demanding friend of my parents from South Africa, in his wooden cupboard door export business. An absolute control freak, a man who tore you to pieces each time he did not understand that you had you own way of thinking. It was short-lived but again I learned many things. One of which was not to be like him. I learned what it was like to work with someone who did not have much respect for other people. They build up all sorts of stressful situations and saturate their own blood with chemicals. It led to a heart attack, during which he told me that he saw another world. This was surprising coming from him; I knew exactly what he was on about, but did not want to share his story because I knew he was not a person who would change and learn from this experience. Commonly called an NDE (*near death experience*) [5]. Sadly, in early 2007 he collapsed on a golf course and passed away. When I heard the news, I instantly remembered back to the time when I was staying at his home in South Africa for a few weeks. He shouted at his Zulu house cleaner, who put one ice cube too many in his coffee. He asked for two and got three. This memory upsets me to this day. These experiences seem to all have a purpose for my journey upriver to higher consciousness.

He had dismissed me from the job because I just could not meet his expectations. The moral of this for me was that I was not a 'yes man' – I had my own brain, albeit, supposedly chemically short. However, my grandma had given me £1500 as a contribution to a deposit on a flat. I took out a mortgage and bought my first flat. He was superior at being ruthless and I was superior at being a caring person. He will no doubt have drifted to the lower astral planes where he will learn from his mistakes and one day, who knows, maybe reincarnate as a more spiritual person. I hope so, because deep down, I did like him and secretly admired his calculus as well as every member of his family, all of whom have the largest hearts on the planet. R.I.P.

I wonder if you knew that every time you hurt another soul
You made a hole in your own
It will be life as a tea strainer, on the lower astral planes

Chapter 18

First sale of business
Or
Do not use the Loo

I had now made contacts all over the UK and I had very good relationships with every one of them. There was nobody who would not give me credit and everyone loved to chat with me on the telephone. I had met another boy my age whilst working in that short-lived job for the demanding family friend. This boy was ADHD and if you could add another letter to ADHD I would make it the letter W, for wacky. Ian was severely afflicted. He was an orphan and it saddened me greatly to hear this. He had an Uncle who did a lot to assist him but sadly Ian was like a clockwork motor. If you wound Ian up to do a job, he would go 100% to the detriment of everything else. This is true ADD. Uncle Jay was always there when Ian needed help. Himself also a nutter, in the wood business and had suffered a few heart attacks, despite being young at the time. Ian and I were in our late twenties now. I called Ian and asked him to leave Jay. Ian and I could buy and sell wood together for the building industry. I felt the time was right to do this; Ian and I could easily run the business on our own and my experience with business had taught me hard lessons about practicality. My flat became our office. We had a table and a fax and two telephones. I was offered a parcel of tongue-and-groove cladding from someone in Birmingham and sold it to someone in Manchester. This was my first deal and was enough to pay a few weeks of bills. Ian and I thought that it was a good place to start. My calculus was sharpening; it did so when my brain chemicals were bubbling up with excitement. I saw this in picture format, as a numbers game. All we had to do was find suppliers of T&G [6] in Scandinavia and call up as many of them as we could find in the phonebook. This paragraph is very important with regard to ADD. You see, to us nothing else mattered. We were hyper-focused on making this happen, no matter what. I called the Finnish embassy and obtained seven names of factories. Each one wanted to supply but there was one particular factory, which was family-orientated, new and needed a market. I ordered a 40 ft lorry load to be sent to a North London warehouse. Ian and I, two ADD people, called everyone in the Manchester Yellow Pages and in one week we sold the whole lot. We paid four and a half pence a foot and sold at six pence a foot. My folks came round one day and saw us working. My dad said that if our eyes were lights, we would look like a road works sign. Ian twitched his eyes more than me, but I was twitching other little muscles in my face. They said the energy was bursting out of us.

After six months, Ian's Grandma died and he inherited a two bedroom flat. We wasted no time moving the office in there. We had sold over four lorry loads and the business was growing like mad. On many occasions before we moved to Ian's new flat, Ian would arrive at mine with wonderful news of a new order. My flat was on a hill and he would get out of the car whilst it was still moving, forgetting to put the handbrake on and leaving the car rolling downhill. I had to run out many a time to pull the handbrake up. He would not listen. He was immersed in excitement and spoke at 100mph. The business continued to grow and we moved into proper offices. My dad was tired of dentistry and was suffering some sort of depression through it. What a feeling when he decided to come and work for me. This brought us a little closer.

Our customers were the independent sector of the market and I wanted to move into the chain stores, but Ian was not this kind of material and not best suited. As it happened, Ian started slipping. He had just married a complete nutter. She would explode at him and break things on him, like her hairbrush. I begged him to see the light but it was impossible. He wanted to be mothered, he could not hurt a fly, and he sank and sank. She told him he could do this business himself and learn more without me. My heart sank. Nobody could get through to poor Ian, as slowly his outlook changed. He only shaved every three days, he did not wash his hair, and he developed psoriases and flakes of skin rained down onto his shoulders and arms and then his desk. This was ADHD (W), you cannot break through the conscious barrier; his heart wanted to be with me, but his soul was sold to the devil with the red hair. Some forms of ADD hide other disorders (*comorbidity*) and when those problems are very severe, the benefits of the ADD brain are lost. I knew I couldn't help him, and I certainly couldn't continue running a business with him.

Meet Rico, a man who sold out to the largest chipboard supplier in the UK. He was tinkering around and I asked if he could come and join us to do the chains. He loved what he saw and I found him fascinating. Little did I know that I was taking on board, not an ADDite but a sufferer of OCD (*obsessive-compulsive disorder*). This person was a psychiatrist's dream. He was great fun but paranoid about almost everything. He had constant loose bowels through nerves and frequent visits to the khazi were necessary, whether he made a delivery or not. During his single days, I got a sexy young woman into the office for him. It was one of my ex flings. She kissed him on his lips. He went bright red and ran to the toilet. I followed to see what was up. He had his tongue out and he said, "Do I have a rash?" I said, "Come off it man, she only kissed you." He wore three condoms and I am sure he was one who believed the religious Jews did it through a sheet. That was Rico. He had a very good presence in front of buyers and spoke the Queen's English when needed. He could fling a yarn and was very good in bringing the chain stores to us. We had now bought a warehouse in Yorkshire. We were importing from a Scandinavian-owned mill and helped pioneer the pre-packed, shrink-wrapped, cut-to-size timber into the UK for retail. This kicked up a fuss with the traditional sector that wanted the goods processed in UK sawmills. They threatened us and they threatened the factories, but to no avail. Extinction of the British mills began, not only because of us but because other people joined into the bonanza. ADHD led the trend. We pushed the boundaries, others followed.

One day in the office, the toilet was blocked. We knew Rico had strange habits, one of which was continuously washing his hands, every ten minutes. He wiped his bottom with yards of paper in the belief it was never sterile enough. He would deny that the constant toilet blockages were because of him. One time we all went into the toilet, including my dad, who said, "How come there are footprints on the seat?" Rico looked as amazed as we did. He even suggested that people from outside the building sneaked in and used the toilet. Any excuse was given to satisfy the question. It was a mystery but we were going to solve it.

The plumber arrived and said, "Please do not use the toilet for 15 minutes." "Only 15 minutes?" Rico piped up, "Oh…that's fine…. no problem."

I knew his exclamation was just a facade. The plumber went off to the floor below the toilet, as that is how he accessed the pipes.

The telephone rang for Rico. It was a buyer of a major chain store. The buyer was angry because Rico had arranged a delivery to their largest store; a new store and it had not turned up. I could hear his guts churning. He wanted to wash his hands; I could hear the tempest in his brain, crackling like firewood. This I wanted to see. The normal ritual was: run to the loo, then wash hands, go again to the loo and then another big washing of the hands. Rico's OCD got the better of him. He bolted to the loo and said he was just going to wash his hands, as the plumber was still working on the pipes underneath the toilet. His face was stern and worried and these expressions told the truth of the visit. He was grimacing and clenching his cheeks. He went into the toilet and locked the door. Three minutes later he emerged, glowing in a bright red color. He said nothing. He did not have to, I knew, my dad knew, and evidently the plumber was the last to know as he ran upstairs screaming with soiled paper all over his head and shoulders. Apologies were not enough; this was serious. A huge fight almost broke out. My dad ushered them out of the office and we had to pay a laundry bill and an extra fee on top for the plumber to finish the job. Peace was conditional on sending Rico home for the day.

Once it was over, my dad, Ian and I waited for Rico to pay his next ritualistic visit. We three took turns going on our knees and peeking under the toilet door. We solved the footprint on the seat mystery. Rico had another secret ritual, when cleaning his royal bottom, one foot was placed on the ground, and the other was on the seat. He must have believed this was the best angle of attack in order to obliterate the little critters.

Our business was heading for trouble with an obsessive at the helm with me. Rico had bought 50% of the business. A life of hell ensued. We had overstocked on own-branded product for over five groups and our inventory was just too big for the turnover we needed. The competition had picked up and we owed a fortune to a Scandinavian government-owned mill. They stepped in and took us over. I was forced to resign because I had lost all heart. Rico stayed on until they stabilized it, then for some reason closed it down. Another lesson learned, but it could have happened to anyone, I was sure of that.

By this time, I had a Jaguar XJS, a house in Hampstead and cash in the bank. What did I gain from this that would help me on my journey? I went to Finland and Sweden many times. I learned about sustainable forestry. I spent weeks at a time with the forestry department learning about their methods. I learned about the mixing of species when replanting, such as Birch. I understood the difference between redwoods and whitewoods and the processing of the timbers. I got to understand that the planet could pump out wood for industrial use, yet with clever management you could replant and keep this process on an even keel without damaging the forest. It became clear that efforts were moving ahead in the direction of extracting the most wood from each cubic meter. Only branches were left to fertilize the forest. Bark was stripped and packaged for sale to plant nurseries. The edges of the logs, called Schaalboards, where two corners were rounded from the arc of the trunk, were used as roof slats or the bad side would be the underside of wall cladding. The centre of the log too had its use in the DIY industry. The parts that were not too good were reduced to chips to either fire the kilns or be chipped into paper pulp or chipboard. This was a philosophy. Everything possible must be used and every tree cut had to have four more planted. I visited the nurseries and saw the intensive effort to preserve and to reforest parts of the world. I traveled to Canada and saw the same, even in the remote hills of Scotland a local industry had started for sawn timber and the mindset was the same. I believe this was an important lesson for my consciousness, as a good citizen of this planet. Conservation meant value and sustainability.

One weekend I lay on my bed at 3.00pm. I never fell asleep during the day, but I started to think about things. I was thinking about my mental state and my business. I was thinking about people in general, trying to reach my higher self. I had once met my higher self when under nitrous oxide in my dad's dental chair. All interfering thoughts were stripped away. I stood face to face with my basic neurological program. I could reach any button I wanted and pressed a few to see what would happen. A few weeks later, at home at 3.00pm, I felt that calm feeling once again after many years. The robed being was with me, I never saw her as such but she was there. I floated up off my bed. Not my body, but my consciousness or my astral self. I was relaxed and when I reached a foot from the ceiling I bundled myself up into a ball, somersaulted and looked down on myself lying on the bed. I got a real shock and I snapped back into my body. My skin burned like mad. I came to slowly realize that the conscious mind could separate from the container within which we live. This was an important realization and was just a taste of what was to come later.

> *"My room may be a mess, but it's an organized mess. I know right where everything is."* — Brandon Curtiss

Chapter 19

Enter: my wife Jackie
Or
She was chosen for me

As things go, I was not doing too badly. I had money, a hyperactive brain, fast cars and a home of my own. I also had many women; I could not pull them fast enough. The more I got them, the more I wanted. It was an addiction. This activity brought chemicals pouring into my brain. Sex was the new medicine, but in a way, I was not progressing. Each girl was a gem. They loved me and I loved them but only in the sense of friendship and sex. I had no way of understanding a relationship. I did not understand the phrase 'settle down'. Each new girl brought me a new high. The ADHD brain had learned the art of making these girls feel good; feel wanted and made them want me. I had funny stories for them. I made them laugh. I had the most beautiful women in town; blondes, whatever. The good-looking guys were able to get them on first sight, but me, I had ways of luring them into my sphere of influence. My magic tricks and spoon bending were the greatest puller. I had techniques that Houdini could only wish for. It was easy.

At the age of thirty I started to wonder about my future. I had had a few girls jilt me so I was a little wary of attachments. I had gotten engaged to an airhostess, but could not go through with the wedding. She was not a 'wife'. I did not know what a wife was, but I needed someone who could raise children with me and be a help in keeping a stable family. With my unpredictable antics, it was not going to be an easy job for my future partner. One night I went to the squash club and was to be introduced to a girl named Jackie, by a mutual friend. Jackie did not show up, so arrangements were made for me to turn up at her house and meet her there. I had a sense that I better comb my hair, put on proper clothes; make sure the colors match etc. However I knew I could not sustain this type of behavior. I rang the bell and the door opened and about twelve inches below my line of sight was this girl. She was looking at me and I looked back. I urged using body language to make sure she opened the door so I could get in. Already, I saw she was cleaning, picking things up, moving things out of the way and so on. What do you expect from a Jewish girl? We got talking and she was very much a softly spoken girl. I just seemed to sense that my dimensional friends sent me here, because everything felt so natural. No tricks, no jokes, no effort, everything seemed to relax me and I knew my genes could be safely handled and that it felt right. A few weeks later Jackie was off to Israel for a holiday. Apparently I called her every day, and drove her a little mad but within three months we were engaged and soon to be married. How's that? I never saw it coming, but then, neither did you.

One of her first encounters with my ADD was when I asked her to go buy some suppositories; I had had a few polyps removed from my posterior exit hatch and the doctor said I needed them. I was grounded for a while due to the pain. This little joke about polyps lasted a few years, but after three operations I was absolutely mad with the medical profession, who knew how to collect a few bucks but nothing about after care. They also never mentioned what to do when the polyps grew back, so I decided to take matters into my own hands. No easy task, as they are located in a very difficult place to reach when adding acids and then trimming them with a scalpel. Jackie found my secret paraphernalia hidden in the attic. I had structured a bicycle mirror at an angle, a rig with lights and magnifying glass, sterile materials, and I would disappear into this room in order to cut and remove and manage the eruptions of these polyps until they disappeared. It was a success. The ADHD brain had won another round of the battle with the "Oils".

I do feel sorry for anyone else who has these problems because nobody in the medical profession manages your rear end for you. It has to be improvised by you. I guess I should have patented this contraption.

Jackie found me tough going but we were quite happy. She spent a lot of time talking to my parents about my past and me and about my strange behavior. Her parents seem to have more faith in me than anyone else. Garland's mother and now Jackie's parents. This was a feeling of great comfort. What it meant was that the more I was supported as a person, the more I could do, because that old self-esteem syndrome did still remain. It was hidden, but nevertheless still very much there. That being the case, I needed positive encouragement and my new in-laws gave me more than enough of that. Life started to take shape. I enjoyed the wedding and I enjoyed meeting her side of the family, but then anything new is a novelty.

Ways in Which ADHD Undermines Relationships

- *Impulsivity: difficulty thinking through consequences of actions. "He/She doesn't think before she acts."*

- *Need for Stimulation: high stimulation activities in beginning of relationship. Later, relationship becomes boring. "In the beginning he was attentive to my needs, now he seems as though he couldn't care less."*

- *Conflict Seeking Behavior: one way to get stimulation is by subconsciously provoking arguments. "If I say black, he/she says white."*

- *Forgetfulness: appointments, where you put things, people's names, etc. "He'd forget his own head if it weren't screwed on tight."*

- *Poor Communication Skills: difficulty with listening and verbalizing. Brains are racing ahead to next thought. "He/She never listens to what I say."*

- *Lack of Organization: piles of laundry or paperwork due to distractibility. "Even his piles of papers have piles of papers."*

- *Poor follow through: difficulty completing tasks. "He/She never finishes anything he/she starts."*

By Amy Ellis, Ph.D. San Diego, CA—2003

I prefer to distinguish ADD as attention abundance disorder. Everything is just so interesting . . . remarkably at the same time." — Frank Coppola, MA, ODC, ACG

Chapter 20

Andrea
The first ADD UK charity
Or
Born again, the fog clears

I mentioned briefly my sister Andrea. I said that there would be a reason for her in this world and a very noble one at that. Her second son was born with various problems, one of which was Asperger's syndrome, but the other problem, clearly ADD/ADHD.

Anyway, it happened that one day Andrea said to our parents that she was sure that I had ADHD. I was approached quite diplomatically and told that I need help and that I had a strong possibility of being ADD. AD what I asked? It was explained that there was a certain Dr Musgrave in Bristol, a psychiatrist, and that they had made an appointment without my permission. I had learned to live with overloaded raw nerves and low self-esteem and was already set in my ways. I knew how to pump up my brain chemicals with sex and food, which was a new terrible source of self-medication, and if I acted the fool I got laughs, so who needed a quack? Psychiatrist was a very stigmatic word. It meant, "You are mad".

I could not imagine having to lay back on a couch with some hooter talking to me and then injecting me with stuff and maybe separating the two halves of the brain, splitting my consciousness into 'me' and 'him'. I was assured that my new obsession for food, thanks to which I was gaining weight at the rate of a kilo a week, would be solved. "Just go and see," I was told. Oh dear, I was losing faith in myself again. I thought I was sort of stable. I finally agreed to go. The next week my folks took me to a country mansion, 100 or so miles away. I sat in the lounge area waiting to be called. Dr Musgrave took one look at me and said, "You are it". "What?" I said. "We will do the test anyway but your sister is correct; you are not only ADD but also ADHD." I asked how he knew. "When I saw you, you were slouching into your chair. You were twitching and you were rubbing your hands together, a sort of anxiety" he told me.

"Tell me," he said, "Do you often interrupt people?"

"Yes" I said, almost before he finished the sentence.

"Are you impulsive in your decisions?"

"Yes" I said.

Dr Musgrave seemed to know me very well. He read me better than a fortuneteller. I spare you the details because I do not wish you to use my consultation as a reference for any of your problems, better that you go to a doctor and get checked out if need be.

"I am going to put you onto Ritalin [7] and we'll talk every day at 5.00pm so I can monitor your dose and see if you need more or less" The good doctor told me.

"Fine," I replied

I immediately popped one into my mouth and we said goodbye. We left with me feeling a little skeptical. Half an hour later, I felt this knot undoing itself in my stomach. It slid open, more and more. I had this amazing, relaxed feeling in my gut. It was incredible. My gut must have been tensed up for over 30 years. Next thing, I felt the edge subside from the rawness of my nerves. Now, I had more capacity in my mind with two less things to worry about. My brain felt alive, I wanted to run, I wanted to get outside and feel what it was like to be on earth. All this was new. I could think and could feel the urge to twitch was still there, but dulled. I was truly born again. A fog, which had lain heavily over my mind, was lifted. I never realized it was there. I tell you how I felt. Imagine if your whole life, you'd carried 50lbs of bricks on your back and had a pair of stockings over your eyes. One day I removed them. Each step you took, you would use the same amount of energy but spring forwards twice as far. This is how I felt. I did not have to exert so much energy in thinking. I did not have to obsess over nonsense, I did not have to slouch, and I was ready to go into action. My mind had power, the power of which I will come to tell you and you would not believe. Dr Musgrave said that my brain did not produce enough dopamine, a neurotransmitter, and Ritalin has the ability to release your dopamine in even doses. Now all he had to do was monitor me and set the levels. Wow, this was something. I was ready for business.

At this time, my father in-law had been consulting for some Chinese Indonesians. Sadly, soon after he began this venture, he passed away. An ex heavy smoker, his lungs could not cope any more and one lung had collapsed. We watched as the doctors confined my father in law to a ward, which I have since called the 'write-off room'. Convinced that he was not to recover, he did not. Over the days we watched all the occupants of this ward disappear one by one, as they passed away.

One night we went to see him in that room. One lung down, so a pipe was put in to remove air between the diaphragm and lung to allow him to breathe. During our visit he went blue and was gulping for air. I had to scream at the medics to do something. They dragged their feet and acted to remove the air only because we were there. That night he passed away. He passed away because the 'write-off room' was painted into patient's reality as a place where you had no hope, so you did not try. This experience further reinforced my belief that many medical institutions are not looking out for their patient's best interests.

After this sad event, I took over dealings with the Chinese Indonesians. If you think a razor is sharp, try these guys; they could take the milk out of your tea with out you knowing. They were great fun and I learned a lot. Being from Indonesia, they had forest owners in their family. In no time at all we started up a hardwood business, doing the same thing as before, but with hardwood. It grew and grew and I started taking trips to the Malaysian and Indonesian rain forests. I began to see what they were doing with regard to reforestation. The officials were full of promises and in some cases they replanted trees, but in many cases, it was a corrupt environment. From the top under President Suharto, down to the poor guy who parked your car. Before I knew what was happening, the Indonesians loved me. I was their respectable front and they were the source of my excitement. The chief or ringleader was Ferdi, a complete ADD telephone obsessive. An action man who could turn any thought into an action. A man of few words when not on the phone. At any one time, Ferdi would be handling his property business, our timber business and have a host of other things going on. He had the ability to keep people hanging on; always believing a deal was coming their way. He could make promises because he made them happen and money was no object. He did not have much but always seemed to be able to get it out of people.

The Indonesians had 'snared' a Nigerian Chief for whom they acted as so-called project managers. How, why or what they could do for him was a mystery. It was borne out of patter. They had sold him a building in North London, promising returns beyond his wildest dreams, with their in-house architect drawing up scheme after scheme. The Chief would turn up in London a few times a year and in the beginning, they would hire a Mercedes-Benz and I would wear a hat and act as chauffeur. It was part of a scam to let him think they were rich and on top of the world. Ferdi had a pal in the USA, a great guy, Caucasian, who was in on most deals because he was involved with a bank. It was money on the side and we were great pals. He and I would laugh at Ferdi's antics because Ferdi never saw the funny side; he was so serious. On one occasion, I had to wear my hat and bring the car to the front door of the offices. The Chief and my pal the banker got in and I drove them all to North London. Upon arrival I got out, opened the door at the back and let them all out. When my banker pal got out, he tipped me 50 pence. We sniggered between us. That was the last time I was prepared to waste my day for their benefit. It was back to business as usual. I made a few more trips and after a while understood that my share of the profit was diminishing but the business was increasing. I looked at the expense list; all Ferdi's costs. That man spent money like it was water. He deducted everything he could. I told Suwandi, the other Chinese partner, about this. Suwandi was a very shrewd and cunning man, motivated by money and trickery with not a kind cell in his body. A small man, with the behavior of a fox terrier, with a brain like a computer. In no time we agreed that I go on my trip to Indonesia and upon my return the new company would be set up and we would start running. Cut out the others. In this case it was justified because of Ferdi's antics and because Suwandi had not had any return on his investment either.

Suwandi set me up to meet his colleague, Sunterman, in Jakarta. We had great fun together; traveling up the rivers in motorized canoes, into the jungle looking at the forest. Wild and dangerous it was, at this point I got violently ill and was hospitalized in a military hospital in the jungle. The hospital was on stilts and the walls were bamboo. The Doc was in military attire and brandished an old glass syringe with a thick needle. I was so weak from diarrhea I could not really speak and certainly could not resist nor question the sterility of the needle. I heard kids looking through the walls of the hut where I had been placed, left with only my pants on, saying, "Orangutan, orangutan." This was because of my hairy chest and back. I passed out and woke up a few hours later on the back of a Land Rover. Sunterman was with me, holding me like I was his brother, clearly worried. I had contracted a tropical disease from having ice in my coconut milk. The ice was not sterile and contained bacterium and when it melted, it infected my gut. I slept for three days with intervals where I was woken and given charcoal tablets and water. Eventually I was a new man. I would pop my Ritalin pill and be on the ball once again. At the same time, a cousin of mine was filming in the Thai jungle. He was a film producer, the same age as me. Sadly, he contracted a similar tropical disease and passed away. He was Michael Katzin, whose name is on the credits of various films.

Breakfast in the logging camp was salted boiled eggs; rice surrounded by flies and various nuts and cooked veggies. We headed up river on a motorized canoe. This was Kalimantan, or what was called Borneo in the past. It was amazing; however we had to watch out for submerged logs. Sunterman explained how the hardwood logging system worked; how every group of companies was given a quota of land to log and then had to leave it for 25 years to regenerate. On top of that, they were only allowed to fell one log per set amount of land.

Most of these laws were sincere to the rest of the world; however their real system was totally different. Under the Suharto regime in Indonesia, of which Kalimantan was part, there was a commission run by a crony of Suharto called Bob Hassan. Everyone feared him. He was the president's right-hand man. He ran the commission. Bob had the whole game sewn up. The lungs of the world, this beautiful rain forest was totally in his control. All the large Timber groups were allocated millions of hectares for logging, upon which they had to follow the reforestation code. A certain amount was paid to Bob Hassan's organization in advance. The logging was not properly monitored nor was the logistics properly thought out. When each tree fell, it smashed away other trees and saplings and if too much was cut in one area, the soil was degraded by the sun and erosion took place after rainfall. Roadways cut into the jungle, caused more damage, which can only be appreciated from a flight into or out of Samarinda or Balik Papan. The Dayak tribes set up small stalls near the camps, massaging or selling trinkets. The logging groups set up cities in the jungles. Huge generators were sent in to power these towns, which housed the workers, who processed the logs in newly erected sawmills and even worse; chipboard and particleboard factories. The sewerage is not treated and pollutes the streams, the animals are hunted; monkeys captured as pets for the workers. An orgy of destruction takes place until the area is logged, and then it moves on and repeats the cycle all over again. Horrific. The result of this destructive process is the diminishing rainforest, which is on its last legs for regeneration. Unless this process is controlled or banned, the earth will shake off her fleas, as she did with the Tsunami. This was rumored to have been caused by the oil companies' fields in Sumatra which take out all the gas and oil from the earth's crust, causing loss of pressure underground which is suppose to keep the subterranean rocks and sand stable. It is logical. Take a football and pump it up. The outside is firm and stable. Take the air out. The outside becomes flimsy and collapses. Strangely enough, very recently I did read a report that made the same claim. If true, it's frightening. After this precious lesson of forestry, I was too deep to get out of the business. The best we could do was to sell to the Green importers who needed documentation to prove that the forested areas were complying with the rules. We did our best to bring the groups to Asia and to make the authorities aware of the paperwork needed which guaranteed the deforestation was all above board. Over time some of the Timber Groups seemed to have made a little progress, but to be honest, I saw only a fraction of the proof and chose not to believe them. As with all corruption, shit rolls downhill and the fallout is widespread. Suharto fell and so did Bob Hassan who went to jail. We never heard anything more about him.

Back in London, Dr Musgrave would adjust my medication. Every day he would call and ask me how I was feeling. He would adjust the dose until most of the anxieties were gone. When he felt the dose was too much, he'd reduce it despite this leaving me with some discomfort. In summary, 75% of the rawness had gone and most of the peripheral anxieties. My powers of concentration were really sharp and at times I did not know what to tell Suwandi. He certainly noticed a difference. He could see me challenging him. He was the moneyman, he was the one who held the supply chain, and you did not want to get into trouble with Suwandi. He was ruthless. A man whose brain worked on pure logic. I watched him once deduce the outcome of the first war with Iraq. He got it all spot on. He predicted Saddam would send his air force to his enemy, Iran, for safekeeping. I learned a lot about logic from him and I think this got him worried because in no time we were running into conflict. It was his ego versus my popularity, both in the UK and in Indonesia. I kept the lid on things for a while. In the back of my mind, I wanted to have some extra security. With my new brainpower, I joined the Institute for Surgical Chiropody in the private sector and studied at night for nearly two years. I was secretly receiving glowing reports and achieved some A grades for my course work. When it came to exams, I fell apart. I suffered from fear of failure. This was sad but I just could not take any failure and did not continue. I retained the surgical equipment and books and continued to read on. This was an amazing achievement for me, being able to read study and concentrate for the first time in my life.

After being one of the pioneers in bringing the green issue regarding forestry to the attention of the retail chains, and explaining all the local systems to them by virtue of personal experience, as time went on, I was amazed at how this industry took a huge leap into doing diligence over buying timber from sustainable sources. This is part of the culture of most timber furniture retailers in Europe and is getting stronger in its doctrine as time goes on. I had played a major part in this industry, at great personal risk.

> *The Star visitors gave me a practical lesson in the importance of the rainforests and its ecosystem. I understood its vulnerability, saw vast areas of deforestation from the air.*
> *I began to think of the rainforests as the lungs of the earth, then thinking back to the lungs of my late father in law.*
> *Destroy the lungs and you destroy life.*

Chapter 21

Enter: My first Child

All this was new to me. A pregnant wife, breathing exercises baby talks and so on. I could not really get a grip on all this and more so, I was bored stiff. My wife looked comical. She was eating pickled things. Her maternity clothes were funny. I recall feeling that I was only a kid and should not be exposed to all this but then of course maturity was not on my side. One day, Jackie's waters broke and I had to rush her to the hospital. Upon arrival we were told it would happen within hours. The hours led to more hours and I got a craving of my own, for a curry. This led to many complications because I was out for quite a while. Finally, upon my return it started to happen. The gynecologist wore Wellington boots and overalls, which seemed very strange to me. When my first-born came out, the doc said he needed help and called me to man a manual pump. It was connected to a sucker, which was placed on the baby's head. The whole affair seemed mechanical, until the little guy popped out. That was it for me. Emotion took over.

The births of all my three gems took my breath away and I struggled to understand how I could be holding a part of me, how did I get to this point? Learning new smells and not liking new sounds or my enforced sleep deprivation. However, they all enriched my life in their own unique way. I look at their features and match them to relatives dead and alive. I live for them. When one of my babies was in his car chair, he came with me to drop off my daughter at school in London one morning. I undid the car chair and carried kid and chair into the school. On the way out I was interrupted by a friend and ended up chatting for a while. I got into the car and drove off. After a few minutes I realized I had left the chair with the little fellow inside it on the pavement. I turned back, faced many puzzled onlookers, popped him back into the car and drove home. Learning to be a father was sometimes a tricky process.

Yes, two of my three are ADHD

One of them recalls waking up whilst floating downstairs towards the kitchen accompanied by several hooded entities, heading for a bright white light outside the back of the house in the middle of central London.
He does not like to discuss it.
He described the entities to me prior to knowing of my encounters.

Chapter 22

Depression in the UK
Or
Why don't you go back to South Africa?
Or
I Hate Your Brussels Sprouts

I began to see that Mr. Suwandi was not a very ethical man. I do not mean to put him down because after all, he did bribe the Indonesian Bank and obtain us many millions of dollars with which to import wood. In addition he was the keeper of a huge Indonesian Group in the UK and managed their funds and trade, some of which found its way into our business. He never had his name on anything, always his brother's name, who resided in Indonesia. We had made some money together, but there were certain things I was not happy with. Any arrangement or joint venture, there was always another pile of funds aside for us both. This caused the rot to set into the wood. One day we found that our buyers had grouped together and flown off to Indonesia to buy direct. Our business went down to nothing. I began to get worried and my feet started to sweat, I could not sleep at night, it was terrible. It was something to see Suwandi's family cut us out and deal direct with our buyers. A bunch of soulless thieves. Nice to our faces but ruthless to the core. I knew this would happen but I was not in a powerful enough position to keep the business honest. Suwandi held the reins. I was sick to the core. The essence of Asia is short-term thinking; take now before someone else does. A hard philosophy for me to get used to.

Suwandi asked me to come to a sauna; we sat and talked about Feng Shui. The master came and told us to go to an Island and spend money so we wouldn't lose money. We flew off to Cuba and had an amazing time. To see Suwandi as a human being was great. He was charming out of the office.

In Cuba, Suwandi suggested we leave Havana for a few days and go to Varadero, on the coast. This we did and we were told upon arrival we could stay at anyone's home. Just knock on the door and they give you a room or the entire apartment. For US$10 we got an apartment. The owners gave us the key and told us we could stay for one night. We went out for dinner and came back rather tired and went to sleep. That night I was thirsty and tried to go into the kitchen. They had jammed the door, not locked it but pushed a kitchen unit against it. The door to the kitchen was next to front door, our only exit route. I heaved on the door and it gave way as the unit moved. Suwandi and I walked into the kitchen when suddenly, there was a rush of sound and an object lunged towards us. We screamed and shot back out the door. A chained retarded mute was in the kitchen. He must have been the son of the owners. His legs chained the poor thing. He was very badly disfigured; half elephant man, seemingly ragingly violent and we did not know the length of the chain. We were terrified. The whole night we did not sleep. We heaved a unit in front of our door praying for the morning to break. When at last it did, we had to find a way to get out. We had to undo many locks and fasteners and we did not want to tackle the monster. The fear was amazing; in fact it gave me high. The Ritalin plus the fear equaled an amazing feeling; such focus, such clarity, that I managed to spring the door and we rushed out, passing just yards from a sleeping monster on the kitchen floor. We headed back to Havana to get ready to fly back to the other reality. Cuba was an amazing place and I have to say this because the more I was exposed to people like Suwandi, the more I was led into different world. Here I was, experiencing different countries and cultures, hearing opinions that were contradictory to what the establishment wants us to believe. I started to realize that the media and politicians were some sort of repeaters, telling us only things that others had told them. They may never have experienced what they had heard, they certainly didn't question it. They just passed on what they wanted us to know, in order to keep us in check.

Before I leave Cuba, I must add that we decided to go on a guided tour. When the coach arrived at the destination, a hill overlooking the sea, the Cuban tour guide faced us and said, "Is that not beautiful?" meaning the view. He was facing us and everyone said, "Wow, what is it?" He turned around to see what we saw, a huge glowing light coming from the sea, bursting upwards into a rainbow of two or three colors. He stammered and said that was not what he wanted to show us. My opinion is that this was an underwater ET vessel of some sort, intentionally throwing up this very bright light to amaze anyone who peered into it. I realized that not all flying objects use our airspace, heck no; there is 75% more sea space in our hydrosphere, and our oceans are very deep indeed. Our shipping lanes are 20 miles wide, so imagine what else is down there.

Ivan T Sanderson, a prolific USO investigator during the

1960's, published a book over 30 years ago called Invisible Residents. *He concluded that underwater submergible objects:*
a) Came from space and took up residence many years ago in our oceans/hydrosphere.
b) Were here, in the sea long before modern man came along.
c) Were real and they are here navigating our oceans.

Back in London I was contacted by a crazy chap, nearly seven foot tall called Nigel. This next series of events leads us into the electric appliance business. Nigel had a factory that ran out of money and we could buy it for a song. In doing so, we learned a very painful lesson. With no experience at all in the electric appliance business, we went to Birmingham to see the factory. It turned out to be not much more than a shed. Many components were being assembled by old ladies. No testing at all; just banged together and sold. But then we never knew about testing and before long, we ended up in court. We took over the business and in no time we found that Nigel had stolen most the parts from a previous owner of this factory. We made the loss good for the owner of the goods on condition that he dropped any charges. A week later over forty thousand pounds worth of parts were stolen. Nigel denied it and we could only claim on insurance. I had a soft spot for Nigel. He was ADHD and had pathological mental problems. A big heart, but a background of *"having fallen through the net"*. I knew instinctively if he were treated when he was a kid he would have been fine today. The system dealt with poor Nigel as though he was a criminal. I guess he had become one. This was the difference between Suwandi with his logic and me with my soul, it became like oil and water, more so each day.

Someone had been electrocuted and the Trading Standards had served a writ on us. The goods had been held under a court injunction.

Nigel disappeared and we found that he lived in the local mental asylum as a patient, coming and going as he pleased. It was all on my lap. The barrister and solicitor did not want to handle the case. They said it was a clear-cut case and I would be in serious trouble. Suwandi had given a budget behind my back that was clearly not enough for the legal profession. Suwandi was well hidden as usual. Now what? I spent every day contemplating this court case. I dreamed it, acted it out and finally got a mental picture of all the people who would be there and a picture of the proceedings. I must tell you that this was the first time I had ever been taken to court. My brain started to work on two things at once. All of a sudden I could work and also handle the rerun of the court procedure and all possible events. I was amazed at myself. I got to the point where I had made a template of the court proceedings, which I firmly established in my ADHD mind. There were the people, the Magistrate, the Trading Standards officer, the shopkeeper and the chap who had been electrocuted.

The day came. Suwandi went to Indonesia, highly concerned. I was ready and I went up to the court. The duty solicitor asked me why I did not have any legal representation. I replied that they had deserted me for one or more reasons at a rather late stage of events but that I felt competent enough to handle it. He advised against it because it was serious and could lead to severe penalties. My capsule kicked in to create a power of intense focus. I was set to face the greatest challenge ever. I went into the courtroom and was directed by the clerk of the court to sit in a designated area. I explained I had no legal representation. The Trading Standards officer came up to me and quietly said, "I will nail you, you bastard."

I wondered why. He had a job to do so why take it personally. I asked him and he replied that I had changed the dates so many times for the hearing and I was a crook. This upset me because I cared for him and I cared for the guy who got a shock, but had since worked out from the charge that it was impossible for him to get a shock from the way he described the incident. Yes it leaked water, but no electrical contact could have taken place in the water. I whispered this to the officer but he just ignored me. This was sad. It was a farce. The officer wanted his glory, the electrocuted who did not suffer any shock wanted to claim for suffering and injury and the shopkeeper had broken the injunction and sold the rest of the goods and I was in the dock, perhaps rightly so.

The magistrates walked in and the charges were read. The wife of the electrocuted was weeping crocodile tears. What a joke. The Trading Standards officer gave an account of the situation and I was allowed to question him.

I asked, "Did you know an injunction was served on the shopkeeper?"

"Yes," was the answer.

"Are you aware that he had sold the goods against the injunction you arranged?"

"No," he said.

"If no, why did you tell the court that you went back several times to the shop to take further samples, you must have seen the stock diminishing?"

"Er, well, uh," was his answer.

I questioned the shopkeeper and in no time I had backed the shopkeeper and officer into a corner and showed that they had both acted against the injunction of the court and were in full knowledge that dangerous appliances were still being sold by the shopkeeper.

I told the court that I had all the papers to show them that the components were stolen from our warehouse and someone else had sold them to this shop and that there were reasonable grounds for doubt. The Trading Standards department objected strongly on this point; despite having had their case cracked wide open by my defense. Now it was time to deliver the well-rehearsed *coup de grace*. Remember there were two kinds of gift boxes with two different pictures. I knew which one they had presented in court. I had the other one in my hand and it matched the sealed version of ours, sealed by a testing authority and held by the court. The two were similar but not the same. I said to the Trading Standards officer, "Look at your appliance sample, look at it very carefully. Is that the same box you saw in my office and in my factory? Now think carefully before you answer, it is important because the shopkeeper cannot provide an invoice from us relating to this stock and he has sold the remaining evidence. I ask once again. Is the box sealed by your department the exact same as the box in my warehouse and in my office?"

"Yes it is, I am sure," came the reply.

"Very well," I said, coming in for the kill, "Your honor, look at the sealed box in your clerk's possession which is mine and look at the one held by the Trading Standards officer. Obviously different, the pictures of the appliances are not the same. It is obvious that my components were stolen and a new box was made. I rest my case your honor."

The officer went bright red, the crocodile tears were now real, and the electrocuted man's case was dead. The court acquitted me of all charges and paid my expenses and loss of earnings. The officer threatened me privately outside, swearing vengeance. I took it on the chin, not fazed. I had won, I felt great and now it was time to move on.

As I got into my car and drove through the streets, I felt that alien female presence again. I looked up in the sky above me, and a huge aircraft flew over, like nothing I had ever seen in my life before. The hair on my skin rose and felt prickly from the excitement. I found it hard to swallow. I do not know what type of huge craft that was, and I guess will never know but I drove home as a victor ready for the new debate on my future.

We closed the factory. By now we knew enough about appliances and their problems and so we decided to import from China. We met a character from China at the Birmingham show. We showed him the appliance and he said it would be very easy to make. Appliances had never been made in China at that time. We didn't hear from him till five months later and by that time we were limping along, partly selling wooden doors and partly trading in bits and pieces for shipment to Indonesia. His name was Richard, a typical Hong Kong trader. He said he was ready to supply appliances and he brought a sample. He copied our sample to perfection. Now using the legal knowledge that Tom Barnes had taught me, I arranged for an exclusive agency from him covering most of the tea drinking countries. This was the only way I thought I could tie him down in the event he tried to take our customers. This was to be a good move as Richard did try to take our buyers. We stepped in and bought a strategic share in his factory. Richard had his eye on the stock market. Later he shipped so much rubbish to us that we nearly went under.

The new plan was set. He wanted to float but we held shares and the exclusive marketing agreement. (Thanks Tom). One night in Hong

Kong, Richard handed us a cheque in exchange for our shares. It was enough to pay for our own factory in China. This was the new plan. We headed back to London to make our plans.

We made several secret trips to China and the way we hid it was Suwandi's idea. The old airport in Hong Kong had a side entrance, which met the exit inside the building where the passengers came out to greet their families or people who'd come to pick them up.

Each time we came to HK, after a week of doing our own surveying and setting up, we'd go to the airport, sneak in the side entrance with a trolley and pretend to Richard that we had just arrived. This enabled us to earn an income buying from him, whilst we were getting ready to open our own factory. An amazing and funny experience. Boy, did I learn a thing or two. There was no doubt, we checked out China and we did our homework, we would have to invest in a factory and have someone run it.

> *"I see myself as an intelligent, sensitive human, with the soul of a clown which forces me to blow it at the most important moments."* — Jim Morrison

Chapter 23

The break - in and robbery
Or
You can steal but you cannot kill me – I know your mind

Things were exciting now. I felt we had a good plan and it was nice to have a target to work towards. We would be free of the problems at home and we could buy cheaper without headaches. Then we would set the UK market alight just as I did with the Softwood business, with Ian and Rico the paranoiac. It was just before Christmas, by now my three kids were born to Jackie and me. We were renting our house out during these tough times and stayed with Jackie's mother, my mother-in-law in a huge home in St. Johns Wood. I stared back at my sojourn through time; I carefully measured the growth in my knowledge and experience, and dreamed of the next exciting step. One evening I came home to an empty house; Jackie would be back with the kids at about 6.30pm. I took off my shoes and kept the socks on. The front door entrance area inside was tiled and slippery but the lounge was carpeted.

There was a ring on the doorbell. I thought it must be Jackie and padded through the hall. I opened the door and three hooded men burst in. I tried to close the door but my socks slipped and these gangsters kept pushing and winning the tug of war. The realization of what was happening was shocking. Three burglars masked and armed with knives and me slipping and sliding trying to fight them. Of course they won. I was thrown to the ground, bleeding, and sat upon whilst the others robbed the place. The week earlier it was reported that two people had been killed during this type of robbery in the area. The attack was vicious but there came a moment of clarity. Half in this world and half in another, I was somehow able to reason with them, and the final blow was not delivered. It was threatened however, as a cord was placed around my neck to drag me upstairs. My air supply was nil and I was pulled like a bag of dirt upstairs and kicked into position. They gashed my backside with their knives until I told them where the valuables were. My hands were cut open and bleeding. A plastic bag was put over my head and again that clarity made me able to reason with them and stopped them strangling me to death. My hands were tied with telephone cable behind my back. I heard the door downstairs open and Jackie calling my name. They warned me to shut up and not make a sound. I could not make a sound in any event, I was choking somewhat. I snapped the cord with brute super strength *(Police said it was the result of adrenaline)*. I loosened the cord around my neck and I screamed, "Jackie, run, RUN!" The hoodlums bolted downstairs and tried to snatch my kid from his mother's arms, into the house but Jackie got free and ran with him into the street, screaming. The neighbors in St John's Wood did nothing; in fact one neighbor *(who'd lived alongside the house for 20 years)* asked who she was. I smashed the window open and went out on a small ledge, three floors up, screaming for help until the police were called. The hoodlums ran for it. The police came and the ambulance that day was on strike. A police car took me, bleeding, to hospital and I was stitched up.

This gang killed another old man two weeks later. They were under surveillance and the police knew who they were and found some of the family silver. Like all things, they were never caught but the detective told me I was lucky. One of the burglars was a psychopath and blew a shotgun in a pub once. The detective again told me I was a lucky man and had a lucky family and I was. I was lucky for many reasons and this was another notch on my belt of experience.

In moments like this, facing death or violence, there appears a doorway to consciousness; you can enter it and take control of your higher self. You are able to tip the possibilities, the difference between a severe beating and a violent end. The ADHD brain moves into a special place, no crying, no begging but a crude form of warped logic in cracking the situation. In a sense, I could say one day I expected this to happen to me. We know the possibilities and we know that the chance is always there. That is our world and it is a place where we push the boundaries, but sometimes the boundaries push us. Do I forgive them? Yes of course I do. They were victims of their ignorance. As in Kaapi's world, everyone has the capacity to be good or evil; it just depends on which side of the fence you are standing. Being in the wrong place at the wrong time is a matter of timing, not always within your control. My advantage is that my mind is wired into the multidimensional universe; it allows me to influence events during any slice of the fourth dimension. Once inside this bubble, clarity arrives, all movements become like strings on a violin. I reach out and pluck them very gently till they play my musical notes. It then goes my way.

I recall an English literature lesson at school when the phrase below came to mind.
To reach the flowering of the spirit
One has to go through Self knowledge
Desperation
and
Corridors of light
I think it was DH Lawrence.

Chapter 24

Return of the radiant light beings
Or
Out of body experience

A few weeks later, we had all gotten over the incident with the robbery and come to terms with it quite well. I was starting to dislike being in the UK and my memories of Africa kept sneaking into my mind. I was missing those old days of hot weather and friendly people, going to each other's fridges, and entering homes without knocking. Somehow, I felt this was a cold place to be. North of England they were friendly, but in the South, they did not want to know you. I would go for dinner to people's houses, friends of Jackie and the food would be awful. There was no food culture as such, sure, you could gamble on a restaurant; sometimes it was OK and sometimes not so. I started becoming a sociopath. We went one night to a friend of Jackie and after the meals I was asked, "Did you enjoy that?" My immediate reaction was powered by remnants of ADD, "No." was the reply

"Why not? What was wrong"?

"The Brussels sprouts were overcooked and the meat was tough," I answered.

This later broke into a very heavy argument.

"What am I to do, live a lie? The sprouts were soggy; you need to take pride in the presentation and texture of your country's food".

After all, I knew a lot about food. I could cook and garnish very well. The British beef was so tough you had to chew it over an over. Each time during these outbursts, I was told to go back to South Africa. My standard reply was that if I did, there would be many workers out of a job since I was now an employer and not a Cigarette sales representative or a runner for someone else. I had an opinion and I was not going to compromise the answer.

I started to see how society had its rules all laid out and how people would follow like sheep. To me, they were rituals. You have to always be polite and say the food is good, despite the risk of a second serving of overcooked veggies being slopped onto your plate.

The 'Oils' sip wine, talk of art galleries, and then comes the ritualistic words such as "fruity" or "rich body" and so on. The linguistic comments for Art were amazing, predicting the state of mind of the artist. Words such as "his tempest" or "sort of" this and "sort of" that and at the end of the day a game show on TV finally revealed the painting to have been done by a chimp. You see folks, being ADHD we 'Water humans' concentrate on the bones and build the fabric of life and the 'Oils' ride us and paint in the illusions, as witnessed by a chimp. They like to be seen to be correct, doing the right thing. Even to the detriment of fellow man. Please note that the feelings in my words supersede the importance of being socially correct, saying the right thing, or wearing the right shirt at a function or having to say the food was good. Sorry but remember we build the bones of the planet, we set its direction and push the boundaries so the 'Oils' and others may swim in the lake of our vision. There is no vision in a chimp's painting or in a soggy Brussels sprout. That night after the dinner party, Jackie was somewhat dejected. I realized that I was making her life quite difficult because she was an old soul; her spirit was the type you could believe had been incarnated millions of times. She would never hurt a fly. She is so warm and has deep feelings for others, yet I put her through these incidents, not without shame but nevertheless with strong fervor. I know a flake when I see a flake.

We retired to bed. I was quite tired and we dozed off rather fast. At 3.30am I woke up bathed in a blue light. It was crystal clear, harmonious and relaxing. I wondered where the light came from and how come I had 360-degree vision around the room. I tried to close my eyes but I could not shut out the visual surroundings. I began to realize that I was having another out of body experience and I did not feel any fear or panic. Many occasions I had woken up during the pulling out of the body, or the return to the body. It is a terrifying experience where you are paralyzed but conscious. I normally stopped it progressing but here I was already out and it was great. Next to me appeared two radiant balls of light. They glowed and soon took the form of a human. The feeling of being in their presence was unexplainable. I was in absolute awe, star struck for want of a word. Their existence seemed to vibrate at a different level, not explainable and therefore in a sense, not reachable. They exuded a kindness, warmth, whilst gently summoning me to follow. The glowing was beautiful and their telepathic inferences, not words, were reassuring. I can tell you what happened exactly.

With one being of light on either side, they seemed to hold some part of me, perhaps my arms. I felt so warm inside and so cool outside. They gently led me into what I suspect was a dimension of hyperspace.

The flow of movement reminded me of being on a cosmic escalator. All was glowing around me. Imagine being bathed in a liquid made of light. (*For some reason, it reminded me of the way lighter fuel feels on your hands, a liquid that is chilled, wet but dry*) They took me right into chilled bright white light. They were crouching down, almost as though they were on their haunches. I seemed to already have the knowledge on just how to react and how to handle my state of mind. My access to my cosmic download was so easy. Everything I wanted to know was there for me. They took me through this transparent hyperspace, behind the scene of human life, right into its matrix but from the inside out, if that makes sense… Rather like looking at a stereo set from the inside of its cabinet, then traveling around inside it and seeing all the works that go on in the back of the system, but from time to time peering through its gaps back into the living room, which acted as a point of reference. I then realized that I had become some form of light. Light removed from its earthbound container in order to enter this hyperspacial dimension. Through the liquid light we traveled in what seemed about two seconds of relative earth time, from my bedroom in St John's wood, London, to my living mother's house in Edgware, North London, a distance of about 4 or 5 miles. However, remember, I was on the inside of the matrix so I did not see a house; I sensed the quantum fabric of a house. My brain browser was interpreting this chaos into meaningful and coherent sense. Suddenly the beings pointed to a series of dots, black dots inside floating bubbles. The dots vibrated, sometimes in unison, sometimes erratically. This was my mother's living soul. I mentioned the importance of these black dots earlier in the book. My mother was in deep trouble. This was her life force spinning out of control. I watched my mother from the inside of the hyperspacial matrix, I saw the beings fix or manipulate the dots in the bubbles.

After the job was done, they peered at me; I recall the eye like structures glaring from the blurred edges of the light from their faces. They were imparting that they had done what was needed and remained in this submissive crouching position. There I was, floating in liquid light, feeling vibrations of deep caring from the beings. I watched their color radiate from yellow to gold to celestial white, shimmering and penetrating. The knowledge capsule signaled that the task was completed. I wanted to see more of their form, their features. I knew that this journey was all coming to an end, but I did not want to leave. What I cannot explain to you is the method of communication. Nor can I really explain to you any more than I have done so far. This was an exoconcious reality and the proof is in the next few paragraphs. Within a second I was moving at hyper speed through hyperspace. From the reverse matrix of life, back to my earth bound container body. When the connection between my light body and physical body took place, Jackie was nearly knocked out of bed by my body's reflexes. My skin burned so badly as though a hundred elastic bands had snapped shut on me. I was just short of screaming out loud, having come back from the reversed matrix of Edgware and watching an event, which was not in our reality. Jackie was holding me, worrying about the old heart, that maybe, I was having an attack. Between breaths, I was trying to tell her to call my mother. Her answer was that we could not as it was 3.30am.

We sat up and waited until morning. We waited and slept, on and off. At 9.00 am, I called my mother and asked her if she remembered anything from last night. She was more concerned at me, my state of mind than of the question. According to her memory, nothing happened. I asked if she recalls chest pains and she said, "Good god, yes, how did you know? I remember now, it was about 3.30am and I got up and I was staggering and out of breath. My pulse was speeding at an uncontrollable rate, then all of a sudden it went away, I can't really remember everything."

I went cold; I had corroboration of this supernatural event. My mother is the second biggest doubter of all my experiences and beliefs; my late father was the biggest. She said it; she confirmed most of what I saw. Over the years, I watched as she tried to rationalize her account of what happened and how she tried to put it into her reality in a digestible format. There were times when she said that it sort of happened, and then times she said did happen, but that she had drunk wine and maybe it was just heartburn or maybe it was a coincidence and so on, to this day. This is the difference between the 'Oils' and 'Waters' of this world, one of whom is entrenched in this controlled reality and the other, swimming free, part of mankind's destiny in our evolution, bringing new awareness from hyperspace and bringing man into a multi dimensional cosmic awareness. My next encounter was also corroborated and we will come to that later.

I had developed an intense interest in things out of the ordinary, things in and out of reality and 'things' that were seen in the sky. I noticed that the reports were always debunked and denied by the US Military Intelligence-controlled mainstream media, (*painters of our reality*) and the 'Oils' believe the debunking, whilst the 'Waters' just know that the truth is being hidden by these ruthless people. The petrol villains, 'Oils' extract Mother Earth's crust insulators, letting the gas and crude oil out, deflating the balloon of terra firma. Tectonic plates slip, the tsunami came, over 300,000 lives lost. The air pollution got bad and infections attacked the lungs of babies and asthmatics, they did nothing. The ozone layer eroded and the radiation came through and increased skin cancers. Alas, they did nothing. The lungs of the earth, the rainforests are disappearing daily, hourly. The 'Oils' continue guilt-free, to rape our reality and when messages from our intergalactic brothers were sent in the form of crop circle pictograms with complicated mathematics etched within them, the 'Oils' told the world it was all done by Doug and Dave. People who believe as I do are ridiculed by the majority as it is simply out of their comfort zone to imagine anything other than what they see. However, some believe religions that state soon it will be the end of days, and if the planet is destroyed, the Messiah will come. There are such people who believe this. The scary part is that many reside in the legitimate government and the rogue government. Which is really more difficult to believe, that in the vastness of the universe we are not the only life forms, or that when the world ends, a Chosen One will come and deem us all Good or Evil? Nothing can be so black and white. Exopolitics was born.

> *"Exopolitics focus on the political implications of an extraterrestrial presence known to clandestine government organizations that keep official knowledge of this presence secret from the general public and elected political officials. The supporting evidence is overwhelming in scope and shows that decision-making is restricted to a small group of officials drawn primarily from the military and intelligence branches of various national governments who operate on a strict 'need to know' basis. The policies and appointments of these officials are conducted in ways that 'stretch' or break accepted constitutional processes".*
> *Dr Michael Salla Phd*
> *www.exopolitics.org*

Medical professionals (*Dr. Richard Boylan, Mary Rodwell to name a few*) were receiving a flood of evidence that the planet is being seeded with new genetically improved kids, with upgraded DNA and spiritual outlook. Metaphysicians and other gurus also share the belief and the anticipation of this recent emergence of the new type of human they call Indigos. They are also referred to as Children of the New Millennium, Crystal Children [8], Children of Light, Golden Children, to mention a few. The UFO community is conducting research into the extraterrestrial phenomenon experienced by children. Their explorations thus far have produced such terms as the New Humans or, more commonly, Star Children. If it were caused by the dimensional manipulators, will these kids be more tolerant, and talented? Will they rise up to head governments one day and then rid the planet of poverty, pollution and bring peace? Is this what ADHD is about? One has to be careful and balance one's views here. There are cases where kids are ADHD, talented, then mistakenly labeled Star Children. In fact, some of them might well be incredible but might have other problems and are never treated. Conversely, however, many ADHD-diagnosed kids might be nothing more than intelligent bored kids, mistaken for being ADHD. A consequence of being upgraded by the inter-dimensional manipulators?

> *"On the whole, human beings want to be good, but not too good and not quite all the time." — George Orwell*

Chapter 25

Leaving the UK
Or
The UK has a divine purpose in giving people a sense of proportion

Neil's journey with Light Beings

I had been dragged by higher energies right through the bowels of physical Earth and through the inner matrix of interdimensional consciousness. I had come face to face with the rawness of human nature during the robbery and during associations with business people. The scars of learning were engraved in my mind and the encounters were very heavy to say the least. I knew it was not over and I knew that in a sense it was just beginning. I began to think that some ADHD could very well be symptomatic of the transformation into being one of the new humans, some of whom were seeded from the 1900's onwards. The fitting of an upgraded soul into an old container, it would manifest itself in people who appeared highly energetic and totally distracted most of the time. To others, they seemed bored and troublesome so, medication in the form of a pill is given to stimulate the brain. Maybe for most this works, but to my mind the best additional stimulation for these kids would be to first of all try, intensely-equipped, stimulating educational facilities. Smart kids get bored easily. Smart kids perhaps already know what the lesson is about and may have processed the info long beforehand. We need to move forewords and co join medication with stimulation of the mind. Do not forget that these kids in the main have suffered severe damage to their self-esteem, so their intelligence or potential is somewhat masked at this time. Let us continue now.

Looking back, I can see how wild I was. In essence, I was a big fish in a small South African pond. By going to the UK, I became a small fish in a big pond. This change served to speed up the growth of my character. The UK has a very balanced political system. A civil service whose model was exported to the colonies and these systems still survive today. In politics, the British are the negotiators, experts at it. Their educational institutions are highly regarded and pump out the best scientists. The UK refined me, helped in setting me up to take on my part in the world. Even though I left the country, mainly because of the weather and overcrowding and the coldness of the Londoners, I know that it is a very well-balanced place and an anchor for the rule of law and is trusted worldwide.

I refer to the innocence of the British people. They know not of the secret societies [9] *and private families who make up the City of London's Oligarchy, controlling the world financial systems. They know nothing of the layers of secrecy, which separate from the public the realities of UFOs and super technology; possibly reverse engineered from crashed ET craft. Nor of the carefully managed media truth embargo* [10] *under a US managed international system of secrecy surrounding extra terrestrial affairs.*

A veil of darkness set over me. I was in the doldrums too long. Buyers had deserted me and I was stuck with Suwandi. He had a hold on my freedom, by controlling the Bank. He knew how to use this power to make me do things for him. I had three kids and I wanted the best for them. There was this feeling that my income could collapse, I had to call Dr Musgrave, I needed to have a word, but found the authorities had struck him off and may have incarcerated him. I went downstairs, in the house, alone and fell to the floor in tears, wondering why I had to have this struggle. Where was I going? How could I ever be able to leave the shores of England, breathe fresh air and take my kids to swim in warm waters, to replenish my spirit in the sun? My dinner parties were full of conflict. Life was in a cage of darkness. This sudden depression caught me by surprise. I called out to the creator and his emissaries for help. I cried from deep within, using a type of deep concentrated thought that would let him, or anyone detect that I was here in London, in the deepest crevice of misery, breaking up and almost forgetting everything I had learned or experienced. I went upstairs and my feet were sopping wet from sweat. I closed my eyes and left my fate to my unseen creator and my friends in heaven. I fell asleep and the next morning, still feeling bad, I left for the office.

Upon arrival, Suwandi turned to me and said, "I spoke to my family in Hong Kong last night. I think you better go and live there in the factory until you get it up and running. We will invest and my Uncle in Hong Kong will invest. Once it is set up, take your family to Hong Kong. I really hope you do not mind leaving the UK."

"What?" I replied, "Er… leave the UK and live in Hong Kong?"

"Yes," said Suwandi, "I think it's you who has to go there. It seems lately you've become more knowledgeable about technical matters in appliances and about other things generally. I trust you and believe you can do it."

I staggered back to my desk with Suwandi wondering if he had imposed this terrible new life on me. My prayer answered the very next day; a real chance to leave. I had prayed for this and now someone or something had already made the plans. I was leaving this place of misery and heading for the sun. My family could follow if I succeeded and succeed I would. The picture was taking shape.

"Suwandi," I said moments later, "OK, after careful thought, I can do it."

Suwandi said I should get ready and leave in ten days. The new investor, Uncle John, would have to pay my salary in Hong Kong, thus relieving our burden of overheads in London. The stage was set. I went home to break the news. It was met by mixed feelings from the family. They all thought I was nuts. How can you just leave and go to China, they asked? Over the next few days, all the family members gave their little speech. Many were distrustful of Suwandi and rightly so. However, I believed that I had been given special knowledge that meant I would be able to use this move to my advantage. All these opportunities are born out of new ideas and higher consciousness. This means, if I want something to happen, I make it happen. I believe that there were other forces involved. I believe that they have always influenced this world and that is how the world works. Quantum mechanics does support this view.

My youngest child was only a few years old at this time. I had a very close bond with all of them. I could spend hours playing with them, feeding their fantasies, making videos, dressing up and taking them on trips to the Zoo or to places like Florida for beach holidays. I wanted them to be able to play barefoot, smell the sea air, or run in the jungle. I told them bedtime stories. My brain was buzzing as my dopamine levels were kept in check *(Skeptics could say I was delusional. However even before the Ritalin days, I was able to tell the kids incredible bedtime stories; they appeared as reflections of my internal visions and memories)*

My main fear was for the youngest. Leaving him for a few months at a time would be heartbreaking. He had to hold my hand and sleep with me when he went to bed and had to see me as he awoke in the morning. The other two kids were already past the baby stage and I knew that I would miss them terribly. Jackie never really knew how much I missed being with her. I found the husband/wife love very hard to express, even until this day. I cannot say "I love you" because in my mind it does not convey the essence of true union between two souls who took the pledge of marriage. She may understand it now, as she sees divorce and separation amongst the backbone of our friends and watched the ruthlessness of it all. Hopefully she sees my essence of reliability despite all my strange deviations, a man who is as steady as a rock. There's a huge difference between a man who gives reality and one who gives just empty promises. A man can constantly say, 'I love you dear' and give extravagant presents, all the while having an affair, or the marriage could still break down. My wife and children are my life, and a simple, 'I love you' can't possibly do justice to how I feel about them.

As the time to go drew nearer, I spent more quality time with the kids. I never left them for one minute. I told them that Daddy was going to China and would come back every two months or so. I found it hard to talk about, because I knew the countdown for the return journey had already started. I cried at night secretly. I was torn between my family and my career. I knew Jackie would have to face the critics by herself, but I had to move ahead and bring stability and a new life. I had to leave the UK and I had to one day get my family out and move into a new happy life. It was my destiny; it was what was wanted of me by my interdimensional friends, the enriching of the soul with experience to be used one day for a good reason.

> "There are many reasons to believe that they (UFOs) do exist: there is so much evidence from reliable witnesses."
> PRINCE PHILLIP
> *Duke of Edinburgh*
> *London Sunday Dispatch, Mar. 28, 1954*

Chapter 26

My new life in People's Republic of China
Or
You will not believe the people over here

The time came. I had to leave at 6.00am for the airport. My youngest, Zak, was holding my hand in a very tight grip all night. He did not want to let go. He thought this would keep me here next to him. I gently removed my fingers from his hand, one by one and went to kiss the other two kids goodbye in their sleep. I left a tear on each of the little darling's cheeks. The older two moved a little in their sleep; they knew that I was on my way. Jackie came with me downstairs to get the taxi and she hugged me and wished me success. Without turning back, I left, not being able to face the images of the little darlings left upstairs who will awaken to find this temporary hole in their lives. Their wait would be long. Mine would be longer but filled with purpose. The plane took off. Tearfully I closed my eyes, popped a tranquilizer, and slept nine of the twelve hours to Hong Kong. Upon landing in Hong Kong, I went direct to the Newton Hotel in Quarry Bay. I was waiting for Suwandi's Uncle, our investor partner. Within ten minutes, he arrived. "Hello, me John" he said. He was so happy to see me. John was an ex-citizen of Laos, whose father was an associate of King Norodom Sihanuk of Cambodia in his youth. John later went to China to University and there he met his wife, Suwandi's Aunt. They were caught up in the Chinese Cultural Revolution and their stories were fascinating. I only heard them two years later because at this point John could not talk English. He used sign language and a few words. He was really exploited in China and worked in a government office doing some low-level intelligence work. Many of his bad habits, which I ran into, were because of the brainwashing he went through, and from seeing people being shot and killed for their intellectual beliefs. Chairman Mao killed millions at that point in time and the strange part of it is that he still has a following to this day. I began to learn that in China, there is a belief system. If you crack that, you have a corridor into controlling the minds of the people.

We sat for over four hours chatting exuberantly. He was an engineer and I was a marketing person and Western. I was a tremendous novelty for John. Under normal circumstances, a 60-year-old like John would put his head down and walk past you, giving you space. This strange conversation that went on for hours was so interesting yet we did not speak each other's language. It was intense. The technical words were the same in English and Cantonese so I guess what we were doing was a mixture of intimation, happiness, warmth and then connecting the dots. John was like a child and I realized that he was severely ADHD, so severe that he came into conflict with just about everyone in China. He could never remember what his promise was, or whom he made it to. He said it was time that I go along alone to meet our other investor, Sanny Yung, a Chinese Indonesian and distant relative of Suwandi. Sanny was over 60, a cross-eyed man who looked like an owl, very kind and gentle and very happy. Sanny had made a few bucks but was as tight as a platypus's sphincter under water. He asked that I come to his apartment. He had strange habits, one of which was not warning you which eye was looking at you and it was very distracting. The other habit was that he always put his hand over his mouth when speaking in case you would smell his breath. It was just his way of being super polite. The habit occurred during board meetings when there were shouting matches. It was strange and he moved his hands at great speed when gesturing. For me this was an impersonator's treasure trove, a room full of ADHD people, all talking at cross-purposes, not knowing who was looking at whom and on top of that, we couldn't speak the same language or understand one another. It was all about who looked as though he knew the most and who would leave the table having gained the most face. The louder you shouted the more of an authority you were. A rule I had to learn fast.

I arrived at Sanny's apartment and he opened the door and placed his head at 45-degree angle peering around the edge. Chinese people do this because they are paranoid that someone else could be standing there ready to rob them. He then gave me a big smile and said, "Welcome."

I was surprised to find that he had two kids of seven and eight years old, extremely hyperactive, ADHD and jumping all over the furniture, completely out of control. Sanny did not try to stop them, I guess he couldn't or he did not want to lose face in front of me. We had to get to the point, because Sanny was to find a factory building for us to rent and I needed to discuss this point with him urgently. I sat closer to Sanny, when all of a sudden both kids jumped onto the couch next to Sanny, jumping and play-fighting when one of them grabbed the other's testicles and squeezed without letting go. The kid froze and mimed a scream, there was no sound coming out of his mouth, only the actions and expressions of extreme pain. It was eerie and Sanny was giving info about the factory and something about how many KVA (Power) we would need, all-important stuff to be sent to Suwandi, but the words did not enter my brain. I was preoccupied with this kid whose testicles were undergoing a severe trauma as his brother now tugged at them. Tears poured out of the boy's eyes; he had lost his breath from the shock and pain. I crossed my legs and ensured that my scrotum was well nested within the safe proximity of the crevice between my legs, untouchable in the event that this was a family habit or even a game. Sanny continued to pour out info and I was stone deaf, feeling this kid's agony, praying for him that the kid would finally realize that his brother had surrendered. At last, he let go and the brother started to catch up with his pain and cried. It was a shriek but Sanny did not hear it. He was more interested that I listened to the hard work he had done and in any event, it was a relatively quiet interlude for him since one kid was down and only one was jumping from chair to chair. The injured kid went out of the room, comforting his groin, when I heard a whack. He had clobbered his brother right in the face and made his nose bleed. The distraction was too much; I was witnessing a Chinese version of ADHD, passed down from the father. It was later when Sanny heard me talk of ADD that he asked me for help and I told him exactly what the problem was and how to get it seen to.

I was very fast becoming a sort of medical confidante, with questions being brought to me by my investors, frequently regarding their inability to have erections and the blocking of their urinary tube, due to prostate enlargement. All this happened because they had heard about me training as a foot doctor, or Chiropodist. One thing was for sure, I was not about to plunge my index finger in to any Chinese orifices in order to check the size of the prostate gland. I had noticed that Uncle John had no toenails or fingernails. I was able to file down the nail bed, which had a layer of thick skin, and painted it with a special topical ointment. I was only getting partial results so I had to treat this fungal infection systemically with pills. Within weeks, I had completely cured this man of 'Hong Kong Foot', a common fungal infection. John had had it for over fifteen years.

I was then to meet the next clown, another investor. He was to be their fall guy, as a sort of hedging of bets when investing. Mr. Wong was a young man in the same building as John. He was a toolmaker, a vital ingredient for any factory. Pressure was on him to make tools at a special price to support the business. Payments were too slow to him and Mr. Wong dragged his feet, thus slowing the project down. He was hammered at every meeting and finally he fell away, no more a part of the group.

My office was to be in John's offices. I wondered why they had not started to partition my office area and was told that the Feng Shui man was only allowing work to begin in three more days. He arrived and placed a ceramic horse by the door, three coins under the doorjamb and for that, he got five thousand Hong Kong Dollars. He had certainly found the route to the Chinese belief system because that is what Feng Shui is about, and that is why you have professional beggars in the street, doing a job relieving the guilt of the Chinese, who know nothing better than to squeeze and exploit because they have a sacred way out by paying off gods. I soon realized that I was dealing with a different culture here. I noticed everyone was always busy, working until ten at night. When I looked at what they were doing, I saw that they were inefficient and just following habitual systems that died in the west twenty years ago. By bringing in computers and removing certain office tasks, they were able to leave at 6.30pm, having achieved a more constructive day in half the time. Hong Kong is filled with people like this. They think that they have to look busy to be busy, even though the work they do is time wasting. There were two points that became obvious. One was 'saving face' and the other was this dreaded belief system.

I spent a few weeks in the new offices in Hong Kong. John had a little room at the back where he had a machine that made flat cable for computers. Suwandi was calling every day to get me to push everyone as we had orders from customers, who were willing to support us. The new factory was selected and it was time for me to go up to China with John, who by now had some new English words, which he seemed to use all the time. One phrase was "No industry" and his favorite word was "sadidy". The first meant "not interested" and the second was "salary".

We boarded the train to Lo Wu, the China border train station with Hong Kong, and I saw John handling an electronic translating machine. In front of everyone he grabbed my left nipple and said very loudly, "Dit da Bread?" (*Is this the breast?*). I tried to make him pronounce the "st" in 'breast' but that ended up as a "d" no matter what elocution lessons I gave him. Therefore, he later adapted that word to "ball" so we knew that a breast was a ball. I saw the workings of ADD in every step I took with John. Totally un-medicated, but sixty cigarettes per day provided his reservoir of dopamine. He would draw on a cigarette for about seven seconds until his lungs were full. He used the seven seconds to get his rush and then to brainstorm whilst he was sharp. He started to tell me how many ventures he had in China and how many people liked him. I certainly did, others didn't. He was charming to me.

We got to the factory and we designed together what each part of the factory would be used for and we arranged our injection-molding tools, which were now ready to go to a neighboring injection factory where they would inject plastic into moulds and make the parts for the appliance to be assembled at our factory. This is where I met Mr. Choy. He twitched his eyes ten times faster than I did and his nose had a special twitch. A man of 60, he only heard half of each sentence before he was distracted by another event in the factory. We tried desperately to pin him down for a meeting. My translator had arrived, a Chinese girl called Pan whom I had recruited from a previous factory. We pinned Mr. Choy down to discuss the methods of the operation. I turned around and John had now gone, distracted by the machines downstairs. I went to find him and brought him back, but now Choy had disappeared and gone for Yum Cha (*tea snack*) in the village with a message for us to follow. All this drove me nuts but that was the way things worked. In China, so many are ADD and so many people are distracted by so many things all the time. Whenever these behavioral habits lead to conflict, everyone has a good shout then everyone puts their arms around each other, giving reassurances of how honest they are and how they will never let you down. After that, it does generally lead to a meeting where everything is agreed. Once we agreed that Choy would quality control the components, pack and deliver to our factory and take full responsibility for the tooling, we all shook hands and let our respective departments know the outcome and their roles in the operation. We pressed the button for a trial run. It all went upside down. Choy did not perform quality checks, saying he'd never agreed to and that we had to bring our people to do it. He did deliver but his people threw the boxes onto the truck and they were scratched, and he would not take responsibility. Yes, many of these issues are a result of ADD. However, there is a more sinister reason too. John and Choy were cahoots, in that John was getting a kickback secretly from Choy on every piece. So John did not kick up too much fuss about returning the goods otherwise his kickback would suffer. This is China. Please understand that this is how China works, from the top, right down to the bottom; from the Government, down to the local governments, to the police and customs.

John and Choy's ADD talent was in their improvisations. It was in the fact that the tools that didn't work got fixed in various ways, like turning the injection mold tool upside down. It was in the way they forged their relationships, corrupt but productive. Our relationship went well, the parts arrived at the factory and we were ready to go into production in a few days. First, we had to have our dormitories, separated from the workers by steel gates. Then came the dogs, and then came the secret exits and entrances. Next came the reincarnation of Chairman Mao himself. It was John Wu; a hidden character, shaped by his life in China during the Cultural Revolution. He built a security wall around us, shaped by steel gates, angry dogs and a rule of absolute terror. He was up early, 6.00am. Nice and kind to me but he would lean over the balcony from our dorm and scream at workers. Froth would spit out from his mouth and his face went red. The carotid artery bulged as this happened and I asked him why he had changed. He took me inside and told me that I did not understand Chinese people. He said, "You have to hit first or they hit you." He said they steal and get up to all sorts of tricks, even kidnapping. I recalled how Sanny Yung had peered at 45 degrees around the door when I went to his flat. He was also caught up in China during the revolution whilst at university.

No food, fear of being framed, fear for your job and fear of being shot. I tried to reason with John that if you try to be cool and teach people what to do and show by example, it would be better. I doubted John could handle things on this basis. This was only the beginning. Two days later, two of our girls had their throats slashed. Not to kill them, but a continuous cut across the throat a millimeter or so deep. They were tied up and dumped at the factory gate. John said, *"Big pobem"* (big problem). The local mafia, in cahoots with police, did this again a few times. A signal that you are in their territory and you should be employing workers through them and paying them a tax. I was angry. John was scared. I told John we had to face these people to stop this insanity or I would go to the police. He said if I did that, they would kill him. Then I said we should go direct to this mafia boss. I was talking with a confidence that I cannot explain. I was prepared to walk into the unknown on foreign turf, but I believed deep in my heart I could handle this.

Finally, we were told that the headquarters were in a particular karaoke bar. We entered and they knew we were coming. A young man also named Choy, no relation to Mr. Choy, was their secret plant. He was a person that John Wu had relied on to locate a factory and to pay the electric company and so on. You can imagine how much of our initial working capital had been dissipated through young Choy and of course how much through the unofficial kickback system of John. Now we faced this new threat.

Three Chinese henchmen smelling strongly of tobacco met us at the door and beckoned us in. Their eyes were all on me, not quite sure that this was what they expected. They could have handled John. My translator was with me. They made us wait whilst they reported the fact that a "round eye" had come along as well. After a few minutes, we were placed at a table, the TV was switched on and fruit brought to us. All put in front of me. John was losing face because of the attention I received. The boss man came in; he could have been out of a Bruce Lee movie. Before he could exchange words, I told Miss Pan to deliver my message, which was simple. Stop or face my embassy's wrath. Boss Man blinked and he told Miss Pan no problem; they were delighted to meet me. They would protect us if anything ever happened. It was as though they had never committed this terrible crime. I did not have any fear as I knew the level of attack needed. I sensed his mind seesawing between anger and tolerance. I guess I tipped it from deep within his consciousness. I felt I was there, just like with Roy John Dove in the days of Kaapi, with my hand on the pulse of his emotions, pulling the harmonics of all the available possibilities of a soft landing. Once we had let all parties save face, and agreed to believe that it was not them who'd cut our girls, and that the visit was one of social essence only, the hugs started and I had made John a useful friend, who would pressure our vendors into taking back defect goods. After a year they vanished, but not before our local government came asking for *lai see* or 'red packet', a Chinese way of paying money in the guise of a traditional Chinese New year gift of satisfaction.

The assembly got off to a good start. The workers were abused and treated as trash and slowly they either left or refused to work to speed. I went in alone and asked them to write down what the problem was. I thought if I had a few hundred signatures all stating the problem was John, then I could have him removed from power and he could remain in engineering. In fact, the papers did come in with John being the problem. Once John, Sanny and his wife heard this, they called Suwandi who flew out to the factory from London and all of them dressed me down. They told me democracy was wrong, it was a Western method of control. All sorts of rubbish spurted forth from these evil little minds; minds that only knew how to keep control by ripping the guts out of the workers. I insisted that if the attitude of the boss changed then the attitude of the workers would change. Suwandi put me in front of the whole factory and screamed at me, "Who do you trust, John or the workers? Tell me!"

I said, "Suwandi, your Uncle is a thief." He ignored that and repeated the insulting and tyrannical questioning. Putting a hole right through my soul, which I swore would be the undoing of him and his Hitler-esque family. "Who do you trust?" He screamed.

If I said the workers, I was on the plane home. If I said John, then the workers were no further forward, but enough pressure from the security system run by young Choy would ensure nobody left, because a few months pay was always held back by the factories to control the workers.

My answer was simple, "John" I said.

I do not believe I had sold anyone out. I would plan the future to suit me. I would see to it that everyone got their justice, good or bad. All the people in the factory, key people, I had very good relationships with. I was fair and paid extra from my own pocket to them at times. I always stood by them and was able to strike a balance between my strength with the key people and the flow of orders from my buyers. The hole in my heart from Suwandi never left me. It dripped rage, every single day. Suwandi later apologized because he knew that I was becoming too important. I was his link of respectability between the East and West. I was his face in front of his family.

The factory was pumping out one hundred and fifty thousand units a month. John's piggy bank was filling, Choy was happy making money, local police, customs, extortionists, and in fact, everyone was happy with what flowed down from the top. Nobody wanted to rock this little boat by starting with me, so I was welcomed. I was now a Chinese Manufacturer and all I demanded was that the workers got three meals rather than two a day, that they got hot water recycled from some injection machines that we bought, and that they were treated by being spoken to and not screamed at. This process took about eight months, but my feeling was that my spiritual encounter told me to watch out for something. Something awful, something that was inevitable. It happens when a rotten soul pollutes the souls of others. I was in the warehouse one evening with Miss Pan, discussing more changes to modernize the management of the factory. John was still crazy and although we argued a lot now, he never reported too much to Suwandi because his little piggy bank was allowing him to import very young sexy girls from Shanghai. He would have a new one every two months; he had money for fun and for his life in China away from his nagging wife in Hong Kong. That night in the factory, John ran up to me. He was pale and started to cry. It is strange to see a 60-year-old tyrant cry. You have to blink twice. He said, "Tonight I die".

With that he projectile-vomited pure blood all over the floor and collapsed onto a chair. A second convulsion occurred and his upper and lower dentures shot out. It would have been comical in a different situation. His face was like a baby. His left arm moved up and around, jerking as the life force drained. His head slumped on his chest and his eyes turned upwards. Blood evacuated itself from his gut up through his nose and mouth and all over the floor. In the West, everyone would come over and help. However, in China, it is about face saving. The workers could not ever see the boss in a weak position. Many just walked past and stared at their papers as if nothing happened. Only Young Choy helped, perhaps seeing the potential that his flow of cash could dry up if his golden goose passed away. I laid John down and raised his legs. He had little time and little blood in his body. We put him on a plank and put him in the back seat of the car and drove to hospital. Old ADHD Mr. Choy had come in, crying his eyes out at the blood. This was strange, beneath all the hate, deception and stealing, there were human beings with real hearts at play here. This told me something. It told me that everyone has the potential to respect and love the next person. It showed me that greed covered this respect for others and it showed me that if human consciousness were able to rise above this, then greed would have no place and what would be left would be care, true care. Choy did care, young Choy I believe cared, but cared more for his cash at times. Miss Pan cared, despite her having many conflicts with John and me. I really loved this person John, at least, the part of him that was good. The other part? I honestly felt at that moment, that if all evil died with John, then he had to go. My higher self stepped in and said, play the role, something is happening here.

We got to the hospital and John was left on the floor, as papers were filled in. The hospital was chaotic, not many patients but miles of red tape and different doctors or staff appearing, each awaiting the arrival of another. The same situation as we had in our factory when we would call a meeting. People disappear. I had enough of this and I screamed at a nurse to get a drip and plug it in his vein whilst they sorted themselves out. John was now unconscious with a very weak pulse, barely breathing but hanging on. The drip helped his blood pressure and at midnight, I had to call his wife. She asked what was wrong and I told her to get here, as she might not have enough time. John, with his eyes closed, grabbed my arm. I nearly hit the roof with shock. His slit eyes opened and he slowly turned his head to me. His eyes signaled Miss Pan to stand back. He pulled me down to his toothless mouth. He looked like a monk with no teeth. He looked as helpless as a baby, with all his power confiscated by the powers above.

"Neo" (*Neil*) he said

"Neo, Neo" again he called my name, "You go back my loom (*room*) and take out the girlo (*girls*) clothing. My wy (*Wife*) coming" then he passed out.

This episode seemed like divine retribution, however John did recover. He had to, I needed him as an engineer to lift me, to help me rise up and to help me win my battle. I needed to use him against Suwandi to ensure I could bring my family, whom I was missing terribly, on this first segment of my trip.

His family thanked me and explained that they believed John had been poisoned. That was rubbish; he had an ulcer in his stomach. His stress caused it and he smoked too much and did not eat enough, or regularly anyway. However, everyone was told that he was poisoned by the managers, a ploy used to further the mind control. This could also have been a veiled signal to me that they were not sure of me at all.

It was time to go home to the UK. I flew back and kissed my kids non-stop for hours and hours. I held them, thinking of the times that I wished I were holding them. We lay on the sofa together, my legs wrapped around Jackie's in a sort of leg lock and I told them all of the funny times. They were fascinated. Suwandi treated me like a king and I played along, but when the time was right, I intended to send him packing. I just couldn't come to terms with his lack of ethics in business and the way he cheated customers. The time I spent with my family was too short. I loved the smell of my babies and I loved to play games with them. Business was growing nicely however, and all too soon it was time to rip my heart apart once again. The littlest saying, "Don't go, Daddy". My reply was, "I have to; I have to do this for all of you. I want you to have every day of your lives in the sun and on the beach, playing with me. I want you to be free and to eat fresh food. I want you to experience growing up as I did in South Africa and not have to endure the cramped, wet and stuffy conditions here."

As usual, the little one slept that last night with me with his hand clamping mine. Squeezing my hand, knowing that in the morning I would be gone. I would miss everyone like mad, and with a lump in my throat, I hated the thought that upon arrival would have to drag myself back into the mayhem and sloppy dormitory, which was my room. I shared it with a rat, which lived under my bed; I'd wondered where my pistachios went. He lived in the ceiling, crept down the wall at night, slept and ate under my bed. I never touched him and he never disturbed me, only ate my nuts. He was welcome.

My next experience was terrible. My loyalties were divided. We had our investors in the factory, Suwandi, I, Sanny and John and his wife. The factory was a profit centre and sold all the production to our marketing company. We made enough profit in marketing but Suwandi would do his milking rounds every time the factory bank balance filled up too much. He wanted our cut of the factory profit. Understand that he squeezed their margins down anyway when we bought from them. This constant greed only causes problems. If you squeeze your partners, they will find ways behind the scenes to get it back and more. On the other hand, it might be that Suwandi believed that they were stealing more than I realized and it was best to grab what you could now. To be honest all this politics took away a lot of faith in this group. Why could we not just sell, make money and let the factory's investors make money too? How could I believe in my relationship with them if we were taking from them? I give 100% honesty and partnership when I deal with people, and when made to cheat them, I cannot look them in the eye. Sanny, John and his wife to all intents and purposes always saw me right. I had no choice, I saw no reason for Suwandi in this group and I told Suwandi I had a new business plan. He went mad on the mobile and demanded I did not bring it up again. Sadly, for Suwandi I did bring it up. Secretly I showed John and it was clear. No Suwandi. He did not add value. He was a milkman, a thief, a corrupter and seller of his soul and he had already dirtied my hands.

John and I planned a new factory between us. We had money and best of all it was over a year since I arrived and the news was great; it was time to bring my family. I had succeeded. After fourteen months apart, their plane landed in Hong Kong. I was there waiting, I had not slept a wink. I peered through the doors ignoring my mobile ringing away. There came a trolley pushed by Jackie, my babies, my darlings, all three were riding on top of the cases looking for Daddy amongst the crowds. I ran as fast as I could and grabbed all three of them and included Jackie in the sacred hugging circle. It was joy beyond your wildest dream, I had them all and I was never going to let them go. They could hold my hand every night and I would be there in the morning. I would be able to take them to the beach the next day, to feel the warm sun and the warm water. They would not have to think about being deprived of their dad and to experience beauty of the wilds of Hong Kong, unbeknown to most people. We went out all the time and people in the street could not get enough of the kids, with their white blond hair and their incredible characters. My kids brought so much fun to others; all three are characters, just like their Dad.

Chapter 27

What is so clever about an electronic unit?

Time moved on and it took ages to plan our new factory. We had to make new moulds and we had to do everything over again. China however, had come down on corrupt officials and corruption in general. Offenders were sent to the local stadium for public execution, as a deterrent. We saw the open-top trucks parading the victims through the streets, their hands tied behind the centre of their upper backs, like the straw-tied crabs in the market. A billboard was fitted to the back of the trucks stating their crimes, a truly horrific spectacle. Men hours away from death; a shattering thought. What if their child had longed to hold their dad's hand, never wanting him to leave, not understanding that he would never return? I asked John his opinion. His answer was simple;

"Must kill the chicken to scare the monkey."

I understood clearly what he meant. During the Cultural Revolution, Chairman Mao's soldiers and secret police had to make an example of people, guilty or not guilty. It was the system and the principle. Scare the people; kill the chicken in front of the monkey then the monkey will behave. A savage ideology, it played havoc with my knowledge capsule, having to look for an excuse to agree with John. That is the Chinese belief system, but how about our belief systems in the West? The Pope and many other religious leaders wear a robe as their official attire. In my eyes, it is no more and no less than a dress. Worst of all, these people are surrounded by many other men in similar frocks. Our belief systems make this appear normal, and we believe them to be saintly. We forget about the numerous court cases over the abuse of choirboys. We do not know about the Vatican's secret police or intelligence agency (S.I.V-"Servizio Informazioni del Vaticano".) or their well equipped observatory, which is 400 years old (http://vaticanobservatory.org/). Your consciousness has not reached the reality of such an institution. Western governments send troops to kill and be killed in the Middle East, in the name freedom. Serve your country, be a true patriot. By the way, freedom is spelled O-I-L. To motivate troops and unite the public for war, you have to create diversions. Create fear and you have a control system for the masses. You think hard about what fear has been created in the last few years, from 2001 until now. Surely false flag operations are a logical solution to perpetuate war and drive your military industrial machinery. If there were no wars, what the heck would those military industrial complexes do with themselves? Create enough fear and you can then control the Movement of Private Funds, and work towards tagging or implanting people with microchips in the name of security. You are then traceable by triangulation at any place on Earth. There goes the freedom and in comes control. People, please see through the cracks, do not be a hippo, everything that is seemingly important is painted in. The UFO subject is painted out.

If we are a loving world, why are we afraid to get sick in America? Why does the black budget, (the budget that is secretly collected from a country's overall income, usually covering expenses related to military research) which is estimated at 1.7 trillion dollars [11], take the first bite of the cake? My friends, consciousness is rising, help is on the way. A medical practitioner, Dr Stephen Greer, founded the Disclosure Project (www.disclosureproject.org). They have videotape of hundreds of hours of testimony from high-ranking military intelligence personnel. They all confirm that UFOs are real and that there is a systemic and deliberate cover-up by government agencies. Robert Dean, a retired US Army and NATO Command Sergeant-Major [12], guarded classified files which showed that government agencies were fully aware of ETs and UFOs in our airspace during the 1960s and 70s. By my viewpoint, and I agree that I have a mind full of cells that supposedly do not manufacture enough dopamine; I see that humanity has been hijacked. Our creator wants us to be smart and think for ourselves. The Good Book may be good but the teacher might not be, especially if he explained it by *killing the chicken*. The winner always rewrites the history books, so take it from me; those pages have been painted in.

As I was about to say, before I interrupted myself, it was about Suwandi's next visit.

John and I had a game plan; we would pretend that we wanted to be consultants in the business and let it be known that Suwandi would earn the most this way. Of course he would agree because of his greedy nature. This was the legal key for me to go, but John was not as predictable or reliable. This trait in his evil character led to his downfall later on, which he fully deserved. When you trade your soul for evil, evil comes back to collect. Our creator does not save us from accidents or natural disasters does he? Religious leaders will always say, after the tragic death of millions, that it was God's will. What a nice guy. It is now time to explain to you the main point of this chapter, for legal reasons, I will just call it 'an electronics unit' from now on. I could have come to Hong Kong to sell furniture or radios, but why electronic units? Most electrical appliances are built on a bill of material basis, plus a modest margin. They all cost the same to make (*within their category*) and profit is limited. It is not the same with this electronic unit. The essential microchips were all patented by one family. The family split up into two camps and had a terrible court battle. Finally they settled with each other and as a duopoly they fruitfully supply the majority of the lucrative industry with these microchips. The patents boost the profits for the component makers. A few years before, a bank had bought a minority stake in one of the companies for an alleged several tens of million US Dollars and recently the whole group was bought by a major Insurance Company for many hundreds of millions more. I hear the cogs churning in your minds.

By default, almost every manufacturer of this electronic unit which has the embedded microchip works for the families, just as we all work for the Inland Revenue. Counterfeiters are dealt a swift legal blow and fear is struck directly into their minds. In over 17 years, nobody had ever been able to get into the legitimate microchip sales business; the families had it all wrapped up.

It was time to once again make it clear to Suwandi that he could go and jump in his lake of arrogance. I told him such. John kept quiet. He had another saying.

"Before you step out of your boat, make sure the other is along side so you can safely step in."

I agreed so, but not as an ADHD human. One needed patience, and I did not have any to start with. I told John that you could sit and wait all year for the other boat to come alongside and I thought it best to rather swim out to it. We had the original factory shipping appliances, with the new factory in the background. The story now changed. Suwandi was gone and John had arranged for a local Governor to build us our own factory and we would have to wait but it would be ours and all we had to do was pay a royalty under the table to the governor, US$0.30 per electronic unit.

Whilst this was going on I asked John, who recently told me that he was a Physicist, could we make the component ourselves?

"Velly velly easy" said John, a common thread in China. Everything seems to be no problem but everything ends up as a big problem. We spent time designing. Others had failed and slowly we began to uncover patents at every corner we shifted. If we could crack this, we crack the industry. Many big boys had tried and failed but two ADHD people were working on this, with all sorts of ideas to bypass the patents. By this time, I heard that a British Engineer, the director of one of the families that we called the Evil Empire, had left. His boss invited me for dinner. He used to keep an eye on me because we had brought him tremendous growth and I was a potential danger. He often gave me money for tooling and special trading terms in the hope I would sit still. An ADHD person sitting still? Come on now. 'Water' does not stay still. Water explores every crack in the road, every bump in the earth and when it hits the roots, the plant grows. I called Marlon, the ex-director and told him of my plans to make the components. I knew he hated the Evil Empire because they were ruthless. I knew they hated him too. Marlon was a good engineer, commercially augmented by his pretty Asian wife. She was sharp. Marlon explained that he had the way forward, because he worked for 14 years on these special components and patents. We were almost ready to strike out on our own, but it would take a long time before we were ready to take on the Evil Empire.

> *"I've talked with people of stature-of military and government credentials and position-and heard their stories, and their desire to tell their stories openly to the public. And that got my attention very, very rapidly.... The first hand experiences of these credible witnesses that, now in advanced years are anxious to tell their story, we can't deny that, and the evidence points to the fact that Roswell was a real incident, and that indeed an alien craft did crash, and that material was recovered from that crash site."*
>
> *"The U.S. Government hasn't maintained secrecy regarding UFOs. It's been leaking out all over the place. But the way it's been handled is by denial, by denying the truth of the documents that have leaked. By attempting to show them as fraudulent, as bogus of some sort. There has been a very large disinformation and misinformation effort around this whole area. And one must wonder, how better to hide something out in the open than just to say, 'It isn't there. You're deceiving yourself if you think this is true.' And yet, there it is right in front of you. So it's a disinformation effort that's concerning here, not the fact that they have kept the secret. They haven't kept it. It's been getting out into the public for fifty years or more."*
>
> *"We all know UFOs are real. All we need to ask is where are they from."*
>
> DR. EDGAR MITCHELL
Apollo 14 astronaut
Taped interview

Chapter 28

Men in black — with long beards
Or
Impossible task

Reconstruction of the UFO's over the IFC No. 1 building in Hong Kong, year 2000

At this time, my family had joined the local Jewish community in Hong Kong. There were many black-hatted members and their Synagogues were full of activities for kids and for the parents. They worked very hard to keep everyone together, despite the fact that the other so-called mainstream community were at odds with the Black Hats. Politics galore but our Rabbi was a master at politics, a clever man who should have been a lawyer. He was a great friend but completely addicted to religion. That is just the way the world works right now. He has done more good than bad and more help than harm and I greatly admire him. My black-hatted Rabbi would argue himself down a one-way street, politically speaking, create a fuss and have to back out again. He was extremely tenacious to say the least. Many of the Black Hats have prearranged marriages, in some cases they are distantly related to each other; due I suppose to the size of their gene pool options within their own world. All of them study the Talmud and other religious books with extreme intensity. What does this mean? It means they are obsessive, praying at certain times of the day no matter where they may be. They do many good things for communities but are not always appreciated. They have short attention spans and always seem to be rushing off somewhere, with a sense of purpose. I liked them because to me, they were crazy, but did not know it. To toast you with a whisky (*12 year old Chivas, only the best*) would be a few brownie points in god's book for them. "Lechaim!" (*to life*), an excuse for exaltation. An excuse to bathe their brain chemicals in sacred fuel. A few drinks and nothing could stop them believing the messiah was on his way, or that happiness was there all the time.

At one point, the mainstream synagogue Rabbi was copying the youth programs of the Black Hat's synagogue. It was murder, my problem was that I was friends with the second in command of the Black Hats; a manic Rabbi who thought eight Lechaims (*blessings given with a shot of whiskey*) was the mark to get his brownie points. He was creative in arranging exciting events for the kids. The kids loved him, with his big chubby body and childlike behavior. They did see him carried home on a few occasions by his boss, the Chief Black Hat; perhaps giving a few brownie points back to heaven, as though they ran some sort of divine coupon exchange program. The second-in-command Rabbi of the mainstream synagogue was also a pal of mine. I use the word pal, because I liked him and spent a lot of time discussing the universe with him. He seemed more open to other possibilities within the universe. I did tease him about his uniform and told him that if he wanted to dress and look like a schmuck, do so, but it wouldn't make me think that he was the messiah, or that he knew any more about the divine dimensions than I did.

So here, we had a situation; both junior Rabbis at each other's throats, copying youth events and both rather aggressive. I was taking my boat out for a day out and I invited the Black Hat Rabbi. I had promised the mainstream Rabbi many times to take him out for a trip but we always cancelled due to rain or wind.

Just before boarding the boat, the mainstream Rabbi called and said, "Hey can I come, I am free today." I panicked, both Rabbis on the boat, both at each others throats, both severely ADHD and there would be ten other members of the community on board, split evenly between the two communities. I did not want a riot. He turned up and both the Rabbis saw each other and decided to sit at the extreme ends of the Junk boat, one in front and one at the back. These are our teachers, our example setters for tolerance in this world, ha ha. I hid the whiskey, and probably scored twenty brownie points for myself with the lord, for using my loaf. I kept moving from the front to the back of the boat in and out of each one's conversation, as a sort of host, to gain intelligence in case they were planning a mutiny. When we got to the outer islands of Hong Kong, I told the captain to drop anchor and we would do a spot of fishing. Our creator has a sense of humor for sure. I gave hand lines to the congregation passengers. I gave rods to our dueling Rabbis at either end of the boat and taught them how to cast. After ten minutes, they looked like anglers. Like the real thing, each asking his master in heaven to give him a fish. I wondered whom does God listen to when two sides are fighting. I do not mean to sound disrespectful, but I believe I show my respect when I use the word 'creator' as opposed to God. This is because 'God' is created by man, to bring him to earth. This is so the less fortunate can perceive him. Used as a tool of fear, in religion to control the masses, by the religious leaders. The creator cannot be defined, nor brought down to earth, but can be experienced, if you can somehow raise your consciousness. So to come back to the question, what does God do when two sides pray to him, in this case two Rabbis asking for a fish? Listen to this.

About ten minutes later, the Rabbi in the front of the boat, minus his black hat mind, screams, "Hey , I got something man, Baruch Hashem!" (*Blessed be god*), "It feels like a huge fish!" Everyone's attention focused on the Rabbi reeling his rod in. With every meter of line it became harder to reel. Suddenly, the Rabbi at the back of the boat screamed. "Hey a fish, a big fish, maybe a shark!" and the attention went to the back of the boat. By this time both were screaming and no-one missed out on the fact that God had helped both Rabbis. After all, they prayed every few hours, they kept Kosher, they set examples, and they said that they had caught fish. God only provides big fish for Rabbis. They both tugged at their lines, puffing and panting, both watching their lines now taking shape into two angles. It appeared that the two large fish were swimming towards the middle of the boat, right in front of their congregation. Divine providence had surely provided them with the best position to witness the catch. The lines from the front and the back of each Rabbi moved to the dead centre of the side of the boat, in the most acute of all angles. The lines seemed to touch as though one had the mother fish and the other had the daddy fish and they were kissing each other goodbye. All of a sudden both lines came to the surface and each Rabbi had actually hooked the other's line.

Their differences were dropped, alas for only five blissful seconds. God gave his answer that day. He gave neither a fish. He hooked them up with each other and told them to both grow up. To me, this was confirmation that their clown-like attire was manifested centuries ago from the ego, as a method of control. How smart is our creator. This seemed an example of the spiritual laws of the universe, cause and effect.

In a talk with the senior Black Hat rabbi, he told me that Hong Kong was a tough place. The people brought to Hong Kong from the Western banks and law firms etc are all the top five percent in their firms, so the standard and quality of person fits into a very narrow bandwidth. It is not a fair and average mix of character but a definite distillation of dollar chasing, some ruthless and some kind, a bunch of driven people who have a different constitution to many other categories of people. They had money. I needed money.

One of the community members, an aspiring leader if you like, ran abroad with his family when SARS hit the Hong Kong people, then limped back when it was over. I started to analyze just what some of the community were really like, bearing in mind I was analyzing the top five percent of the world's brainpower, sent to HK to make their firms and selves rich. One of them introduced me to a tough, clever American lawyer.

"Neil, you must put together a business plan. Then you can raise money in what is called a PPM or Private Placement Memorandum".

I had no microchip, I had no patents, I had no microchip making factory, I had nothing to sell, only an idea on how to make and patent a microchip to challenge the duopoly.

The Lawyer told me to get this done and that raising money was not easy. I must persevere non-stop. I sat with Marlon and John, not quite letting them know that we had nothing to excite people. In any event, the whole of Hong Kong had lost a fortune in the dotcom era and we were just coming out of it with investors licking their wounds. I had come this far in my sojourn, I had endured hard work, attacks at home, left my family, done time in China and now the barrier was money. I figured I had to swim out to the boat and not wait for it. I had to use every single neuron in my Ritalin-propped brain to let quantum mechanics shape the reality around me. At last the 60-page PPM document was written up, showing all the possible returns on investment. I would use this document to dream of my busting the powerful Half Billion Dollar cartel wide open. I would prove that my mind was determined and although I had reading and writing problems, amongst many others, I would see this through. I would do my work in the current factory and I would raise money if I had to knock on every door in Hong Kong. Amazingly, after the first four calls, I received substantial investment from people I can only describe as angels. They were not the people sent to Hong Kong by big companies. These were people who came to Taiwan long ago and when that got uncompetitive, they came to Hong Kong. These were humans, big hearted and very warm

We had enough money to at least do the research and development and start to get the patents filed. It was a hard year. A very hard year, but the light was beginning to glow at the end of the tunnel. When the idea of raising funds was presented to me, my good friend Mango unconditionally gave me the money. In fact, I had to have a result rather fast so that Marlon would feel comfortable and believe that I could raise it. When it comes to calling for money that's when you know if people are serious. Mango just sent it to me. Let me tell you a little about him. If there is water and there is oil, in his case there is "Woil", a definite mixture, the best of both worlds. Mango had a heart the size of a water melon. He was the most stable in the community and a Governor on the board of a Hong Kong day school. When he spoke, he spoke sense. Whenever he said something, it was said with confidence. His families were all nice people and his late mom and living dad, whom I had the pleasure of staying with in Israel once, were just the perfect human beings. Sadly, his mother passed away. She had cancer when I was there, yet I never heard a moan or felt any negativity from her. This summarizes the background of Mango. At times, I often discussed the universe with him and came up with explanations about time and space. Mango, with his big beautiful eyes, just looked up at me and smiled and said, "You know Neil; I am just an A, B, C sort of guy."

Mango accommodated my obsessions and at times I was able to make him wet his pants laughing. He respected authority, but when he was with me and we were both facing authority, I would unpick in public those who thought they were above us. I would give my honest opinion. I would say what he and others were thinking, and watch him blush. I am just crazy about Mango. Little did we know that this nuts and bolts, ABC kind of stability would one day serve to anchor my so outrageous stories. One day Mango was out on the Junk boat with friends and when they returned to shore that night I received a garbled call from Mango. To the best of my memory, it went like this:

"Neil, I was on the boat with Feinstein and er, er others and we saw like lights in the er sky, sort of white but reddish then... well...

I cannot really explain. They were in the sky but flying… I do not know how to explain…what they were because we took pictures and they did not come out."

I said, "Mango, listen up, from what you are telling me, you had a sighting of something perfectly explainable, but without clear info I can't help you. You are not making sense."

He answered rather frustrated, "Neil, I mean they were round light balls and large and sort of… in a V shape but I can't explain."

"Mango, why don't you take me there tomorrow?" I said comfortingly.

"Yes great, for sure, we are unloading a boat at Kowloon at 8.00pm, come along then, I will wait for you." Mango replied.

Now here is his predicament. The Governor of the Board of a school, a co-founder of the school, the son of the founder of many schools abroad. A Managing Director of a huge company. He now sees the equivalent of the Virgin Mary and cannot put it into a digestible perspective and has to go home excited but confused with nobody but yours truly to talk to. He needed someone like me to commune with when life jumps off its sprockets.

The following day I thought I must go and investigate, because I have been obsessed with Ufology, mainly due to the many experiences I'd had and because when I was in Florida on holiday with my family some five years previously, I was mysteriously drawn to a book store filled with UFO books. I bought over eleven books and read them all in the few weeks before we came back to London where I used to live. Is that not strange? I know I am strange but for me, that was bizarre. A few years earlier, I would not have been able to read a page, let alone a book. A few strange episodes occurred whilst in

Florida, but I think it is all too much excitement to cram into this book. I am trying to let the Oil humans read this book and not cause them to be put off by my incredible experiences. The result would be that this book would be confined to the fiction shelves of some street vendor and never looked at again. I swear by all, everything in this book is fact. At 8.00 pm I turned up at Kowloon, as arranged with Mango. The view across Hong Kong's Victoria Harbor was amazing, a clear night and the skyscrapers were lit up with colored lights and designs. It always astounds me when I sit there and stare at that view. Some years ago, before my father passed away, we had both sat and admired the same view together. We'd had one of those father/son conversations from the movies, when he let me know that he was my dad and always would be, but that he'd had hard times with me. We talked of other things, like how I had exceeded his expectations; coming from a man who'd disapproved of me and not understood me as a child, this was wonderful to hear. I thought of all these times as I waited for Mango, so I guess my mind was a little off topic. I was looking forward to the meeting, I loved seeing Mango. He was originally from South Africa too, so this was an important key point to our relationship. It made me sad when he'd told me that during his compulsory South African national service, he was bullied so badly that he considered doing himself in. It is terrible when you are taken from home and placed in a right-winged environment and nobody can or will help you if you are picked on. Some hearts are soft and some are hard. Mango was just a pile of lovable jelly. On the funny side, he told me he went to work with the medics, to avoid the bullying. He knew a lot about medicine and treated many people. Once, he told me, his job was to wheel the bodies into the morgue covered with a white sheet, and when he got into the morgue one of the bodies jumped up and screamed. He said his heart nearly stopped. A friend of his had waited to give him a shock, hidden in the depths of the morgue. Such was the reality at that time for Mango. Anther quick Mango story, before I get back to the sighting, sorry, that's ADD, was when a Zulu came into the hospital with an axe embedded in his skull. Mango and the crew removed it under anesthetic. Three days later the Zulu returned looking for his axe.

I walked up to Mango, who was on the gangplank of a big boat carrying oranges that he had chartered from South Africa. They were unloading the boat and Mango and the Polish Captain were locked in conversation. I walked up the gangplank and tapped Mango on the shoulder. He returned an embarrassed stare, in case I brought up the UFO subject in front of the Captain. I kept quiet and let him continue talking. The Chinese workers were busy unloading and the operation was going well. I turned one more time to face the Hong Kong view and as I did, I saw from the South West, golden bright orbs, each as large as a huge truck, glowing with a celestial light. I have to use this term because light plays an important part in physics, creation and out of this world experiences. The light I am talking about is not like that of a lamp or welding torch. It is a rich, warm, mind penetrating experience; an experience of something that fills you with confusion because you have to explain it. I now know what Mango meant when he tried to describe it. You just cannot. It is awe-inspiring and its richness changes from white light to gold light. They were in a Delta formation which was around a kilometer wide. As I watched, four more chevron or delta shaped orbs arrived and flew around the light beam that was shining skywards from above the IFC No.1 building on Hong Kong side, which I estimate at about fifty stories or 600 ft high. The beam was about half as high again so if I said 800 ft altitude I would be correct within 20%. The ships slowly cambered in formation and flew around the light beam of IFC one, at approx 25kph. No aircraft that

I know of could fly so slowly in deafening silence. No aircraft that I know emits such a godly white light; no aircraft I know is a huge as what we saw that night.

I was awestruck and Mango turned around and shouted, "There they are, that's them".

I could not move for a moment, I was so amazed. Mango turned to the Chinese workers and asked, "Can you see those? What color are they?"

Out of twenty workers about four answered, the rest said nothing. One answer was that they are any color you want. The answers were strange and the behavior was weird. Most of them chose to ignore the lights. I did not understand this since Chinese have dragons, Feng Shui, ghost night, cleaning of graves, and believe in spirits as a way of life. Later when I told my own boat captain, he told me in his 60 years of fishing at sea, he had seen things fly out of the sea and into the air, so flying around a light beam was child's play for him. All his fishing cronies had seen various types of flying objects in one form or the other leave the sea in silence and head into the clear night sky. He was quite matter of fact about it. We watched for hours as our visitors of the sky displayed their magnificence to their fullest potential and sadly we watched them take off to the East. They had left us with a feeling of richness for the experience and only after they'd gone did I feel sick that I did not bring my video camera. After research, the nearest thing I can compare them to were the Phoenix lights in the USA. Recently, an ex-Arizona Governor, Fyfe Symington, admitted that despite him dodging the many questions at the time, he did see the Phoenix lights along with 29,000 other witnesses but was told to keep quiet by the military. Poor Mango tried to tell his wife and he got it in the ear. I told the Black-Hatted

Rabbi and he told me it was a reflection in a window bouncing off pollution. I thought to myself, "Well, that's better than having been told I had seen swamp gas."

This experience happened in front a solid member of the community, it served to endorse who I was and everything I had told people about, in my past. This was a great event, ranking almost equal to the visit of the robed being in my room when I was a little kid. From that moment on, as has happened with many others in the face of the liquid light, emitted from these ships, my consciousness began to raise, my brain required less Ritalin, I could think of things that I could not think of before. I became interested in the bending of space and time and I started to write short articles in magazines. My attachment to wealth was important but not a priority and I think my obsession for out-of-this-world events became unstoppable. My reading exploded and I researched feverishly using the internet and books. My mind was happy but I knew that I lived on planet Earth and I had to focus once again on my work to bring this microchip to market. I had a responsibility to my investors, Marlon had joined the train and we were ready for the journey. The game plan was set. The PPM (Private Placement Memorandum) administered, over 40 patents filed and we had to continue making appliances without the two microchip families knowing, otherwise they would stop our supplies. Marlon was now injecting trial parts. All the tools were ready and many tests had to be made then everything sent off to the approvals board for electric certification.

The patents were a nightmare and if not for a young British patent lawyer here in Hong Kong, it would have been near impossible to navigate our widget construction through the minefield of over 450 patents. Nobody ever wanted to risk that. Buyers did not want to risk buying from anyone else either. The power was just too strong in these families' hands. Only a fool would try to get into this market. However, this fool was tired of working for the families indirectly. They made the money and we sweated. That was the reality, a reality that was not mine. The plan continued, and the Evil Empire got a sniff that I was up to something. Immediately I got a visit. Their clone in a suit, clipboard in hand, told me that he heard Marlon had set up a microchip factory and that I was involved.

"No, absolutely not," I said

"If you do, we will close you down," said the smacked-bottom-faced clone. His boss in the UK had put pressure on him but the shmo had already sold his soul to the Evil Empire and was hooked. Our secret work carried on day and night. A week later the clone called and told me he knew that Marlon was up to something, because they had visited an injection factory in China and had picked up scrap molded parts. As of that moment, all my microchip prices, on which I was dependent on them, went up by US$1. This meant I could not sell, I was no longer competitive. All the big brands asked for their deliveries and I told them I could not deliver because I was a target of the Evil Empire. Sympathy was limited. They wanted their goods. In their heart, they knew not to upset us. They knew I had been in this industry for a long time and was not a person who lay down and died. My brain was stressed. How would I get through this? I had an idea. I went to their largest customer in China. I charmed the boss and the secretary and offered to buy the Evil Empire's components from them, cash up front with a nice profit. They would look good as sales went up, and I would be back in business. This worked well. I had fooled the clone, I had slipped away to be able to deliver and generate revenue whilst we were getting ready to launch our component.

A week later the clone started to worry, he had told his boss I was finished and yet I was still in business. They have the most sophisticated intelligence system that makes MI5 look like nothing. Their clones are all over the world, walking the isles of exhibitions, combing through factories asking questions. Finally a week or so later, the Evil Empire found out that our microchip had been approved and that we'd started to ship. Our company structure and the way we operated made it hard for them to attack us and in addition we had legal insurance in place. All was fine, sales rose and I decided to go to Malaysia with my family for a hard-earned holiday.

Upon my return, the business was going through a growth spurt and needed more funds.

I approached a Russian friend to arrange a loan from his connections. He had cash all over the place. His middle name should have been cash. To him life was cash, and you saved cash by walking everywhere and skipping meals. He was a real Russian, who had friends that might inspire you to cross the road before meeting them face on. That was Vlad, straight hair and a curly nose with a dimple smack bang in the centre of his chin. Every mirror was a stopping point, whilst his hair was carefully put in place by a pat of the hand or a small comb. It seemed like a form of doodling whilst he was on his mobile telephone. If they called him, it was a long call, but the other way round; he would find a local telephone because calls were free. Vlad was streetwise and ADHD as they come, and any conversation which exceeded his attention span was either stopped or forgotten. He did not cut the cake, he stabbed the cake. Nobody made a profit from him, laws were something made for working around and money was not for spending but for storing. Presumably, he had plans to take it with him to the next life. Vlad was able to secure investors and we soon were able to cope with our immediate needs. The families were doing everything to head us off and Vlad saw blood. He did not like anyone messing with me. His plan was simple: scare the Evil Empire to death, and play them at their own game. He would start by getting a few Russian waiters he knew, putting wires in their ears to make them look like Mafia bodyguards. Both Marlon and I cringed, wondering how this would play out.

"Leave it to me, get back to work, I can handle it," said Vlad. At the next exhibition, the big boss of the Evil Empire arrived into the hall, a brilliant, ruthless lawyer who had built his huge company up from nothing, who ruthlessly controlled the minds of his staff, a man who worked in round numbers, a man nobody crossed. The king of the Evil Empire walked past my booth and peered in to see what I was doing. He had several of his clones on either side and they all acted brave in front of their king. Before I could even say hello, Vlad stormed in, his well-built body scantily covered by a t-shirt membrane, muscles bulging and the arteries in his neck protruding and pulsing. His henchmen followed him, wearing dark glasses, wire ear sets attached. They immediately picked up the king of the Evil Empire, carried him into the corner and menacingly warned him to never ever think of starting any battle with us. Vlad and the boys let him go and he returned rather flustered to his clones, who by this time were bright red, not being able to muster up an equivalent weapon in their king's defense.

This incident was followed up by persistent telephone calls to his home, which was located in a wonderful tax haven. We never faced another direct attack. Vlads' ADHD had made a major contribution towards him taking this action without any fear of consequence and it worked. We all laughed because little did they know that Vlad had taken some poor waiters, dressed them up and told them to stand straight to look big. It worked like a charm. We were back in business. Many events unfolded during that time. My kids had grown up somewhat and one of their close friends had had an encounter with substance abuse. I got the news, and I got it hard. My two boys were ADHD and had to be watched. I had to ensure that they did not fall through the cracks. I managed to find out where this boy was and it was scary indeed. I planned to pay some people to help me abduct him and prepare a holding cell on one of HK's outlying islands where he would be incarcerated until he was cleaned up. This was the way I figured I would cure him. I never understood this part of life and whilst I had separated him from his substance, I had no idea that this could only be a brutal temporary measure because things slid downhill and fast. Finally I had him released and looked to experts for help, who managed to drain a lot of cash out of his parents. Psychiatrist after psychologist after specialist, country after country, each medical report was different and each medical bill was worse than the other.

This experience gave us a shock, and I understood just how far you can fall if there is no support for the parents. My sister Andrea helps parents understand just what can happen to ADHD kids and this support that her charity gives has saved lives and taken people off the street. The "Oil doctors" had not understood ADD and its consequences and many of these doctors simply refused to recognize ADD/ADHD as a condition, and set it aside. Her fight against these stubborn doctors was finally won after she went through a long and hard struggle. Her fight continues to this day, and I am prepared to tell my story in the hope that people will become aware and ask questions and seek help instead of believing their kids are crazy, losers or naughty. They are not, they are bright, bored or in many cases lack dopamine and would be far better off being medicated through the early part of their lives, certainly until they finish school. Now that this interlude was just about over, with the king of the Empire chained, we figured that if we could sell at 30% cheaper than the Empire, they would lose US$1 every time we took an order.

One thing we never anticipated was that in patent law, you could register a patent using the priority date (*original grant date or validity date*) of an earlier patent, as long as it was still valid and paid up. This meant that any new patent's priority could be backdated to the earlier patent, thus catching you whilst you had goods already out on the market. This is very unfair, but nothing in our reality is fair, it seems. You have to work the system, something Vlad learned when he was growing up living in Russia. He could see the game and he knew how to ride it. As soon at the new version of the Evil Empire's patent was granted, we were literally almost finished. It was designed to hit our core patent, and then they would be able to do with us what they wanted. They could deal with our buyers and scare them away. Vlad never thought the Western laws were fair and he was intent on cracking this one. We had to look for prior art (*proof that this was not a new invention*). This means you have to look for other similar inventions where this has been done before. He spent eight months scanning the old Soviet Republics. Marlon and I spent the same time on going though patents; we had to find any prior art that could show the families' patents were nothing new. Against all the odds, Vlad found such a piece of prior art. He found it in the Old Soviet Republics, in libraries, which pre-dated the families' priority date. They would be scared to challenge us because the Insurance Company had just paid a huge amount of money for their company.

We met with one of the families in order to find a path forward. For us to keep this info hidden, they would have to pay us. Long and protracted negotiations took place, however they were doing nothing more than gathering intelligence on us. They appeared interested in the business itself; however, a culture of arrogance and sharpness prevented that from being possible. It was back to the drawing board. They then targeted us in the market place, ruthlessly dropping prices, trying to take us out. We fought back twice as hard, using every trick up our sleeves. Vlad really had nothing to add except push us. We were confident that no legal case could be won against us by the family, but the customers were threatened by them and were all scared. The ones who stayed in support of us appeared to be very ADD, very talkative, thinking around the problem and asking questions. The ones who ran away were very reluctant to get involved in the matter at all. Therefore, who did we favor? Of course the loyal ones, because they were thinkers, not because they were brave. They understood the game. They could not be threatened. It was so interesting to read these people and to know them because to me, they fell into specific categories; either fear of consequences or no fear of consequences, of course underlined by a sense of risk and risk management. In this way they measured their risk and helped us push the boundaries once more.

Our growth curve flattened out. The Oils exceeded the Water humans and the propaganda campaign was so strong that our sales could not venture forward en masse as we wished. It was sad and Marlon and his staff in China were becoming dejected. A morally broken sales staff in China is dangerous because word spreads and so does rumor and they started to think we were going downhill. My ADD brain knew that the cartel was obviously too strong but the more I was depressed and the more I dwelled on it the more Vlad would call me and pick me up. Vlad always gave me encouragement, however he always took it back when you had used it, but he did assure me that he was always behind me. He had kept telling me to engage in talks with the other family but we thought that they were not really up to taking on the Evil Empire. They had just completed another acquisition themselves and we thought perhaps they had enough on their plate.

My poor brain was screaming for a way forward. I was under such huge stress with eczema around my eyes, tiredness causing me to sleep late. I would not go out except to work. I had a task to beat or join the cartel, it was a matter of great importance, and proof I was not mad, proof that my friend's parents did not have to remove their kids from my presence, proof that I would not be cleaning the streets. It was not about the money, it was about the confirmation of who I was and that I was no less able than them.

All these points began to stab at me and all the old memories came back. I was now comparing myself to the way I used to be and what people had said about me in the past. My self-esteem was on the brink. I questioned why I had experienced my out-of-this-world encounters with radiant beings and why I had sometimes felt like I was special.

Just as I though things could not get any worse, Marlon called me in a panic. He reminded me that the other family, the ones we refer to as the Gentlemanly Empire, had just filed a divisional patent. First the Evil Empire, and now the Gentlemanly Empire had done the same thing. They had applied and received a divisional patent, a backdated patent on their microchip. This meant we were now under severe attack by the cartel proper. The patent was granted and we had a small window of time with the European patent office to file opposition. The marketplace would hear about it and then we would be crushed out of existence.

We needed prior art once again to show that this was not a new idea.

By some stroke of luck, the junkyard genie must have put a hand in. When Marlon and his Taiwanese wife went to Taiwan for a break, they saw in someone's home an old appliance pre-dating the families' patent; it even had the patent number printed on it. Marlon offered to pay anything for it and in no time he was back in Hong Kong with his prize in hand. Our patent attorney immediately dismantled the item and obtained the published patent application records and an opposition to the patent office was submitted ten minutes before the closing time allowed. With confidence rising, we could see that we had the two major points, which covered the industry's protection; these two points had kept the cartel intact. If the oppositions went ahead, we'd all lose because in no time at all, the Chinese would then begin to make these components at a thousand miles per hour and the selling prices would fall through the floor. It was time to talk to the other member of the duopoly cartel, the Gentlemanly Empire. I had to think about how to make this call. These were the gentleman of the game; hard but fair and we knew each other. I called for the CEO, he was away and I left a message.

A day later my mobile rang and a warm voice was on the other end. "Hi," I said and he asked how I was. I did not have to talk much, the man knew what I was proposing and in true spirit left out all the duelling and replied that we would have a meeting within a week and it would not be in the UK where he was based but in Hong Kong. This was a huge leap forward. Our negotiations were like a bullfight. With slow movements, grace and dignity on both sides. It was a process of reaching the target together smoothly. You would hold out the cape, the idea of our component being a second brand for them. The matador would swerve gracefully, as we both swerved and stayed polite, dancing, waltzing to avoid conflict or arrogance. The matador would wait for the picador to stick his spears into the bull's neck, so we let our soldiers prod each other to see where the boundaries were and how far each would capitulate in a deal. I needed this deal to happen, it was important for me to be party to overthrowing the Evil Empire, who had been so cruel in getting to the top. This was my main objective now, to tear the Evil Empire apart and to let the Water humans who'd supported me become successful, and take the business from the Oils that had walked away from us. I had to ensure that this acquisition paid off for them as well and I wanted to be sure that I could make them the number one market leader.

Was this an impossible task? If I had got this point, how hard would it be to get to the next point? I wanted to do it. If my brain said, "I need you to do it," I would follow the cracks and find the chink in the armor of the Evil Empire's customer base and take it apart, piece by piece. It would be nice to see an Insurance Company, who'd paid mega millions for a microchip company suddenly find that the mouse they tried to step on was able to crawl up its leg and somehow chew away at its belly from the inside. Negotiations continued and a major meeting was now underway in a top UK lawyer's office in Hong Kong. The office has large round windows, which faced the harbor. To my right was my lawyer and to his right was Marlon, with his laptop open, constantly peering at graphs and numbers. Focused to the nth degree. I am not sure he knew what he was looking at. My lawyer was sharp as a razor and to my left, the family's two directors and their lawyer. A 70-page contract was handed out to us all. To be honest, we'd all had it a week earlier but I just did not read a word of it. I pretended to Marlon that I had and he would talk about points but I would dance on my feet and improvise the answers. I could not read even one paragraph; the words appeared to fly around the page and squash up against the next word. I could not hold the letters in one place and was not sure which clause I had read. It sounds strange but mentally I was not really there.

When each lawyer spoke about a point, it appeared as a pictogram in my mind and I could react swiftly and understand. That is because it was read to me and comments from the other parties reinforced the meaning. This was great. However, when a pictogram did not appear because there was nothing exciting about the words or meaning, I would drift into a dream, coming back periodically. In the middle of the meeting, I asked to be excused and left for the toilet. My bladder was so full and I just had to go. The secretary opened a door by tapping in a code on the door lock and pointed down a long hallway. She asked me to turn right at the second crossing. I did and went from door to door until I found the men's room. After this, I came out but turned left instead of right to get back to the hall with the coded door lock. I ended up god knows where. I was trooping up and down, passing loads of lawyer's offices, sometimes once or twice and each time they looked at me wondering whom I was. I was lost; it was as simple as that. I was panicking because a long absence means many things. Either you did more than a piddle or you had another reason for staying out of the room. I came to a fire door and through it, I could see familiar territory. I banged on the glass but the girl could not hear me. I was sweating. The hallways were long and I had done a marathon. I was hot and bothered and upset at being lost in this maze of lawyer's offices. I was needed at the table or so I thought.

A hand tapped my shoulder, it was the secretary.

"Oh there you are, Mr. Gould, are you just looking around our offices?"

"No," I said, "I got lost, sorry." She saw my sincerity and she acted politely, leading me back to the room. I walked in and everyone asked how I was. I told them I was OK just that I went looking for drinks. After half an hour, the clauses were becoming more and boring. A few good fights had taken place but now it was very dull. Two Mainland Chinese helicopters flew past the window. It was soon to be the 10th anniversary of the handover of Hong Kong to China, celebrated every year, no doubt to encourage Taiwan to drop its trousers.

My mind was now on the choppers. I imagined I was sitting in one preparing to drop down the line and abseil onto the ground when a distant familiar voice shouted at me twice, "What do you think of clause 64:2:2b? Neil?"

It was my lawyer and as the echo of his question became louder and comprehensible, I answered, "Those Chinese choppers are a darker green than the usual color."

Everyone laughed, probably because everyone was bored and I was the only one who was able to escape the room mentally. They knew that is what had happened. Their CEO once said to me that he would welcome someone on their team who was good at smoke and mirrors, meaning someone who could dance on their feet, tackle any situation without fear and confuse the enemy. The talks reached a stalemate over various points. Clauses on many points regarding China were very complex and we all had to go home and think. The head of the family had to leave for a meeting in the UK. Our lawyer was to be in the UK at the same time anyway, and negotiations would continue there. After that, they would all be on a week's summer holiday. The wait was frustrating. I needed to tear the Evil Empire apart, protected by the family's patent umbrella.

Chapter 29

Why can't you be like them?
or
Wolves in sheep's clothing

Another ten days passed. I had received word that the lawyers on both sides were going on holiday for a week and my counterpart on the other side was away for two weeks. Certainly, this put further frustration into the equation. The delay meant uncertainty and my brain could not stand not knowing. A person with ADHD cannot cope with being in the middle of something exciting then having to wait. The motor does not turn off. It remains on, scheming and scheming through the night, playing different scenarios through the mind. The framework of the deal had been outlined already and I would be staying on. Whilst this sounds a little strange, it gave me many a brainwave. I could challenge the Evil Empire whilst completely under the protection of the other family's patent. I could exert justice on them for all the things they had done to others in the past.

During the interlude, I heard that my lawyer had to depart to the Americas but would leave another lawyer to handle things whilst he was away. Again, all this served to frustrate me even further. It was important to me that the deal was done. Nobody had ever really wanted me, let alone paid for me. I started to plan in my mind the many angles I could use to ensure that my customers would succeed, and prove them right for having believed in me. I set about planning once again. All was secret, part of a confidentiality agreement and I could not tell anyone. An ADHD person, keeping a secret? How many Chinese would I like to let on to this pending situation that at last I would be there and be able to assist them all to hammer back at the Evil Empire? Keeping it secret, I did, but it was difficult. My family could not coax anything out of me. My wife was getting very upset with me over the weeks. She accused me of not listening to her, turning the TV up too loud, not wanting to go out, not socializing and being inconsiderate. She told me I was really a troubled person with an affliction. It was hard to tell her that for me the deal came first and that I was obsessed with it and could not turn off the motor. It seemed that the engine was stuck in gear and that it would remain so until the outcome was sorted.

During our marriage there were countless times that she told me, look at so-and-so, look how happy they are or look how so-and-so lives, look what they have got and done. I cannot tell you how many times this point came up where she felt deprived of attention from me over the years. In earlier times, it bothered me somewhat but the strange thing was that over the years the very people she referred to, in almost every case and beyond expectation, split up. Countless couples, who were supposed to be soul mates, were on the verge of splitting up and their relationships were held together by a piece of fragile cotton. I guess that although I was difficult to live with, I was reliable as a family man, had staying power and always looked after every member of my immediate family. It was natural to me to do so. I felt their needs and felt their problems. I did not feel anything about being difficult at home with my wife because in truth, I felt that although big-hearted, she could be petty about what I considered minor issues. The fact that she allowed the pettiness to interfere with the quality of our lives meant that, that was her level of perception of the world.. A comfort zone if you like. For me, I was more interested in what was going on in the world, what was happening and where opportunities were. It was either up here, or in my altered states, between dimensions of reality. It must have been difficult to live with me; the toenails on the floor or the curry-stained shirt or the loud TV or the excess passing of wind, were all ADHD signatures. No doubt at all, in some cases I am to blame, but time is passing and age is catching up and life must go on for everyone.

Happiness is always found in next door's cupboard
When the cupboard door is opened, the skeletons fall out.
Your problems sink into insignificance.

Chapter 30

Defragmentation

The following morning I did my ritual. Every weekend I go walking in the Pokfulam National Park. It is a huge park right in the middle of Hong Kong Island. A jungle, as wild as those back in South Africa, and home to many forms of life. My bulldog Siggy accompanies me, as he loves it too. I have decided to write down the begging questions I get from my daughter regarding these walks, because the answers are at the core of the multidimensional brain.

"Why do you always go there every week Dad?" she asks, "You're so funny."

My answer to her is this, "When I see the city, I see everything as square shapes; buildings, boxes, cars, buses, signposts, fruit vendors' tables, roads, windows, doors, steps, lifts, books, computers. Sorry, I do not want to bore you with this but I could go on and on. I know you never thought of this, just accepted it as your reality. Your world is square. This is how you have to live, being exposed to squares."

"But Dad, what has that got to do with why you always go to the Pokfulam National

Park"?

"Wait poppet, I am not finished. I ask you this question, what do the folk in the city think about all day? They are designing, curing people, accounting and so on. Mostly the focus is on money for survival but that is normal, to desire prosperity. Their purpose in the city can be compared to a clock that ticks from nine to five and a wheel that clocks up how many units of wealth can be created within that time period. It is like a hamster's wheel to some extent or a treadmill."

"Daaad, stop it, answer me!"

"Poppet, the universe is chaotic, but it evolves by cosmic laws which operate at quantum level. The universe is filled with stardust and a cohesive force pulls the dust into planets and so on. Chaos is important to note because the brain has a recognition mechanism, like an internet browser, to interpret chaos, to give it meaning by putting it into sequential order."

"Dad what are you saying? You are so fragmented."

"If you looked at Earth from space and listened through a sound amplifier, you would hear millions of sounds all crackling at once. Absolute chaos. The closer you focused with your 'browser' the more meaning it would have. Let us go deeper; we are now over Australia, amidst a huge mass of sound. If we focus the 'browser' on all the telephone calls and eliminate the rest of the chaos, we still do not hear anything coherent, but when we finally reach three or four conversations, we can make out words. When finally, we reach the one telephone conversation and eliminate all chaos, we hear a sensible conversation. Therefore, within chaos, there is order but you have to find it. I demonstrated my point using chaotic sound as an example, but you could do the same with lights, and the same with buildings and so on. You see, within chaos, there is purpose and order, even though you do not always see it. Consciousness strives to give it an orderly sense of purpose."

"Phew, Dad, what planet did you come from?"

"The universe as we see it is chaotic, but it has layers of order defined by the laws of quantum physics. Most of the universe is just not apparent to us because we are wired into a three-dimensional universe of length, breadth and width. The universe is a multi-verse with many more dimensions than the three we are aware of. We cannot see them, just like fish see waves and light at the surface of the sea, and know another reality exists up beyond the water, although they cannot see it."

"Dad, get on with the Pokfulam National Park."

"In order to observe, you have to have senses to decode the information coming in."

"You mean eyes for light, and ears for sound?"

"Yes poppet, correct, those are your sensory input parts of your 'internet browser'. So we are wired into a sector of the universe that can be sensed and interpreted by our 'browser'. Now, evolution is the ability of multi-dimensional consciousness to adjust to complexities that threaten to stop or limit life. You see, you cannot just stop life.

The more the environment that supports life, as we know it, is damaged, the more our collective consciousness will be challenged. So nature brings about special methods to deal with this. To put it simply, weed killer stops weeds for one season, but another seed comes about, resistant to the weed killer and weeds grow again."

"Dad, how do you know about these multi-dimensional manipulators?"

"I am writing a book as you know and I am doing my best to tell people exactly what I experienced in our everyday world. I am doing my best to honestly tell what happened in my extra-dimensional world where I met beings of light and I am doing my honest best to tell people what I do know for sure. I will tell them that being symptomatic of ADHD; I am not limited to a square template of the universe. I am wired into a multi-dimensional universe. I am not Superman, but my 'internet browser' can browse into chaos, be it here on Earth, or in the multi-verse. I can perceive hidden layers of order and make sense of it all. Most folk without a supercharged browser cannot do this. They are focused towards convention in this reality. To them, chaos is not something to look into for answers. It is a blur to them. They simply do not have the will or the required software. This is the most important statement that I will make when I write the book. This is a useful tool for the unscrupulous to implement a mind control system. To create chaos, in the form of terror, religious guilt or explosive diversions, then act upon them in the name of convention. Once you have their attention and have created fear through chaos, you have their heart, mind and soul."

"Dad, come back to your special methods that nature has, to deal with human consciousness."

"OK, I will tell you what my ADHD 'browser' with its extra supercharge has shown me. I have communed with entities, which are not visible by normal sensory perception of light; in fact, a part of you has to go to their reality in order to exchange thought. I say exchange because there are no words to describe it. These are highly developed, disembodied and conscious energies that have been around forever and they all play a part in the propagation of the universe, respecting the free will we think we have."

"What do you mean?"

"My fish in the fish tank think they have free will; they do and they do not. It depends on their level of understanding, which brings us back to consciousness. Poppet, you know that when I tell our family of my very strange happenings, they immediately laugh it off, debunk it or whatever. That is the limitation they have in order to feel comfortable within their reality, to create order out of chaos. ADHD symptomatic people are sensitive to both worlds and seem distracted all the time. They are dealing with mass sensory input and interpreting the resulting chaos into order. They are doing this all day long at both a conscious and subconscious level. The supercharge they have in their brains requires them to be stimulated all the time because of their brain 'browser' potential. It leads to much trouble because the rest of the folk do not understand them. If there is not enough chaos or stimulation, they fidget and become hyperactive and seek chaos. Coming back to these energy entities, they influence and upgrade the square world by supplying new souls attracted to different shapes, if I can put it that way. The more advanced, interesting and colorful those new souls are, the more easily they can infiltrate society and bring about change. This is what evolution is all about. ADHD and evolution go hand in hand. Long ago, there were cave dwellers. Certain characters went hunting and concocted ways of catching prey, took the risks, traveled afar through risky territory. The others gathered berries, planted crops. Here we have two differently-shaped sets of consciousness. One propelling and inventing and the other staying safe and collecting berries."

"Dad, you are making me frustrated, you STILL haven't told me why you go to the Pokfulam National Park!"

"Poppet, I take the dog and I sometimes take you and your brothers and I watch you all carefully. By observing the dog's actions, you would think the dog's sole purpose in life is to wander aimlessly, pee every hundred meters and poop every half hour. However, he is not randomly wandering. He walks through the forest and his main sensory input is chemo sense. He follows lines of scent, which you cannot see. He knows who has been there and at what stage their fertility cycle is at and he marks boundaries for various reasons. He perceives order in chaos that you cannot perceive and to you his actions look random. It just reinforces what I am telling you about interpretation of chaos, and how order is not always apparent to all."

"So?"

"Poppet, at home, I am from time to time, fed information by way of my extrasensory input. It is not easy to explain to you but when it happens, I relate back to the first face-to-face visitation I had, with the robed being, as a kid. It is a continuum of information, a feed into the knowledge capsule that they downloaded into my mind. When I go to the National Park, the minute I turn off the road, all the squares disappear. No buildings and no echo of the city. I enter the bush by way of a path and I see chaos in the form of many shades of green. There are more greens in the bush than there are words to describe them. This fascinates me; the shapes and intertwining of the leaves one on top of the other, many plants huddled together and vines of all types filling the cracks between the available spaces, climbing up the trees and winding around the branches. New vines shoot out parallel to the ground reaching out and swaying, looking for somewhere to grip. I see moss growing between the rocks and fungus consuming the dead wood in the forest. The yellow butterflies always fly in pairs around the violet flowers, which grow on the side of the path. The waterfalls cascade down from the mountain and in every month, they flow with different intensity. Some months they are dry and I look under rocks to see what lives there. Where does all this water come from, where is it being stored? It never makes sense to me. How come the monsoon rains never flush the tadpoles away after a storm? It is because even in a flood, certain rocks cause the flow of water to move less violently, adding some sort of protection where the tadpoles move to. The laws of nature are special. The moon acts in a similar way to these protective river rocks; its density in the river of space bends space to cause the dynamics of gravity and space-time to merge hyperspace and the earth, perhaps to propel the creation of larger life forms. I see large spiders and cannot understand how their webs stretch across a stream; they do not fly. I see an interweaving of branches, chaotic but full of shape, depending if your 'browser' can see what I see. Even the surfaces of the trees and branches add happiness to me, it is all ADHD and I will never kill or remove the beauty that I see. I see the forest not only in three dimensions but also to some extent, in four dimensions. I mean time; I observe it from month to month and I know its quirks and rewards and I know its difficulties, especially after a typhoon or during a drought. I can hear the language of the forest. You see it is not in words at all; it is a coordinated harmony, a song of color and events, a song of life and purpose and it reverberates through my browser as a song of the universe. It is all connected and the connection is at a multidimensional level. That is why I believe I was invited by the energies to observe the multi-verse from a different perspective. My message awakens others."

"Dad, you are funny but I love you."

"Poppet, you are also funny and Mom and I love you and your brothers more than you will ever know."

"Dad? Long live ADHD."

Poppet's world soon experienced a shake up. She came into our room in the early hours of the morning, quite disturbed. She had woken in the night, frozen and unable to move. She had sensed a presence in the room, which had scared her. Although her TV was left on all night, it had mysteriously switched itself off. This was similar to my very first experience of the condition the medical world calls "temporal paralysis."

"It is true that I was denied access to a facility at Wright-Patterson Air Force Base in Dayton, Ohio, because I never got in. I can't tell you what was inside. We both know about the rumors (concerning a captured UFO and crew members). I have never seen what I would call a UFO, but I have intelligent friends who have."

SENATOR BARRY GOLDWATER
US Air Force General
Presidential Candidate
Letter dated April 11, 1979

Chapter 31

Never call anyone stupid again
Or
The caller of names do not know their own name

I would hope that by the time you had got to the end of this book, you would realize just how different people are, compared to yourself. Not only different, but people are involved with your reality only to the extent that you find things in common to talk about. If your belief system is so polluted that you cannot even see out the other end or you cannot see the obvious, logical conclusion, then for heaven's sake, do not call the other person stupid. He might well be sitting there watching you poke around with your white stick, not being able to find your own way around. Imagine that? The more people enhanced with this ability to see past your reality, the less you should get into altercations with them. Do not label them, because if they are ADHD-symptomatic kids, at the beginning of their journey, your ignorance could affect the outcome of their lives during adulthood. If anything, you should be tolerant of them and if you feel a child is too different, perhaps unmanageable, best to get some professional advice. You cannot use a hammer to straighten the nail in this case. My view is that the more frustrated you are with people you do not understand, then the more you need to try to understand the problem. It may well be with you.

Every generation will have different software and in many ADHD kids, other symptoms will mask the real problem. These kids need special attention because in the early days they will be problematic if not attended to, but bet your boots, in later years they will be the ones who can get things done. They will run circles around your methods and will achieve the most in all probability. Remember that the world changes every month, almost, with advancements in technologies and these ADHD people, invariably, are related to these changes. They may be the ones advancing life by inventing these technologies and pushing the boundaries and you might not be in tune with this pace of change. Just think back 50 years and you will see how far we have come, within the visible spectrum, with technology. Then there is the invisible spectrum, the technology not passed onto the world by the military industrial complex, with their secret agendas. The military only now release 'new' weapons or jets which were in development thirty years before hand.

I had to laugh whilst watching a National Geographic documentary how they said a kid with computer-game experience would be the right one to steer an underwater unmanned submarine for attending to wrecks or oilrigs. They would be more adept to manage the controls with fewer collisions than any trained adult would. On the other hand, I am called an obsessive bloke and yes, it has been easy for me to annoy those around me. I am called obsessive and wrongly, so, I deny it. The confusion here is that to me, being obsessive is purely hyper concentration on that which interests me. The problem to everyone else is that they say my obsessive behavior is to the exclusion of everything else. On one occasion, I had a friend who went to see an addiction specialist and whilst I was waiting for him, a counsellor told me that the doctor was obsessive and said that it was a fact that obsessive people get things done. That is the main advantage of people like me, which outweighs most of the disadvantages; we get things done.

I will admit to being obsessive about hyperspace and I enjoy reading up on this subject. To me it is the background template of everything, as it weaves throughout consciousness. My conclusions are that ET intelligent life use the fabrics of hyperspace as their highway whether from star systems or from different dimensions. It does not stop there; powerful thought is transmitted through this highway and disembodied entities swim through it. It is the very life force itself and it is conscious, continuously trying to rise all within it to a higher level. This act of rising is called 'time' and anything that moves through time is called 'life'. Death would be the beginning of the next step upwards to new level, that is, if the soul had been able to enrich itself on earth. If not, well, heavy things sink to the bottom, do they not?

Without exception, every time I encountered an extra terrestrial, although communication was telepathic, the sense of pure acceptance and harmony was the first thing I noticed. I do not want to say 'love' because that word is too simple in a case such as this. They must vibrate and exist at a completely different level and in most cases there seems to be different degrees of light emanating from them. Could this mean that the more one rises in spirituality, the more one becomes light?

On the lighter side, once in London I saw in the newspaper that ET had landed in Johannesburg. I recall it was 2 April 1992. I ran around the house shouting and obsessing, ran up to my wife, and said, "You see, I was right, look here at the article." The article confirmed that a craft landed in a Johannesburg suburb and out walked an alien who introduced himself as Lirpa Loof. I loved the name and I was ecstatic. I ran to the TV to see if there was any word on this matter, alas, nothing.

My wife walked in laughing and said, "You big schmuck, Lirpa Loof is April Fool backwards."

> "I wanted to convey to you my views on our extra-terrestrial visitors popularly referred to as 'UFOs,' and suggest what might be done to properly deal with them."

> "I believe that these extraterrestrial vehicles and their crews are visiting this planet from other planets which obviously are a little more technically advanced than we are here on Earth. I feel that we need to have a top level, coordinated program to scientifically collect and analyze data from all over the earth concerning any type of encounter, and to determine how best to interface with these visitors in a friendly fashion. We may first have to show them that we have learned to resolve our problems by peaceful means, rather than warfare, before we are accepted as fully qualified universal team members. This acceptance would have tremendous possibilities of advancing our world in all areas. Certainly then it would seem that the UN has a vested interest in handling this subject properly and expeditiously."

> "If the UN agrees to pursue this project, and to lend their credibility to it, perhaps many more well qualified people will agree to step forth and provide help and information."

"For many years I have lived with a secret, in a secrecy imposed on all specialists and astronauts. I can now reveal that every day, in the USA, our radar instruments capture objects of form and composition unknown to us. And there are thousands of witness reports and a quantity of documents to prove this, but nobody wants to make them public."
>COLONEL L. GORDON COOPER
>Mercury and Gemini Astronaut
>Address to the United Nations
>1985

"While flying with several other USAF pilots over Germany in 1957, we sighted numerous radiant flying discs above us. We couldn't tell how high they were. We couldn't get anywhere near their altitude."

"While working with a camera crew supervising flight testing of advanced aircraft at Edward's Air Force Base, California, the camera crew filmed the landing of a strange disc object that flew in over their heads and landed on a dry lake nearby. A camera crewman approached the saucer; it rose up above the area and flew off at a speed faster than any known aircraft."
>COLONEL L. GORDON COOPER
>Mercury and Gemini Astronaut

"I should point out that I am not an experienced UFO professional researcher. I have not yet had the privilege of flying a UFO, nor of meeting the crew of one. I do feel that I am somewhat qualified to discuss them since I have been into the fringes of the vast areas in which they travel. Also, I did have occasion in 1951 to have *two days of observation of many flights of them, of different sizes, flying in fighter formation, generally from east to west over Europe. They were at a higher altitude than we could reach with our jet fighters of that time."*

"I would also like to point out that most astronauts are very reluctant to even discuss UFOs due to the great numbers of people who have indiscriminately sold fake stories and forged documents abusing their names and reputations without hesitation. Those few astronauts who have continued to have participation in the UFO field have had to do so very cautiously. There are several of us who do believe in UFOs and who have had occasion to see a UFO on the ground, or from an airplane. There was only one occasion from space which may have been a UFO."

"Several days in a row we sighted groups of metallic, saucer-shaped vehicles at great altitudes over the base, and we tried to get close to them, but they were able to change direction faster than our fighters. I do believe UFOs exist and that the truly unexplained ones are from some other technologically advanced civilization. From my association with aircraft and spacecraft, I think I have a pretty good idea of what everyone on this planet has and their performance capabilities, and I'm sure some of the UFOs at least are not from anywhere on Earth."

COLONEL L. GORDON COOPER
Mercury and Gemini Astronaut
Omni Magazine
Vol. 2, No. 6, March 1980

Chapter 32

The World Is 1 000 Times Faster Than 40 Years Ago
Or
Evolution - a Reason For ADHD
or
Enter: Dr Greer and Exit: Dr Mack

So what exactly is ADHD? My basic understanding is that in some cases it is a pathological medical problem and in others, a supercharged brain, the result of a genetic upgrade, for want of a better word. The two hypotheses become one because the symptoms are the same and the treatments are the same. Both groups find it hard to live without stimulation. Whilst trying to relax over another anxious weekend, at a poolside hotel in Hong Kong, I started a chat with an elderly woman from Australia. She told me she was a teacher but now retired. Of her own volition she remarked how different the kids of today are and how much more advanced they are than when she first began teaching some 45 years ago. The conversation began to explore quite deeply her conviction over such a statement. As far as she was concerned, the way children process information today and the capacity they have is far greater than in the past. She was amazed at their speed on computers and their grasp of complex games and their will to challenge complex games in cyberspace.

I was careful not to influence her thinking with my opinions on the kids of today and whether I thought there were definite signs of upgrading. I did mention that I recall my grandfather some 40 years ago sending letters from South Africa to England and having to patiently wait for the reply. The letters were business deals and you can imagine how long it took to get things done. That was the pace. No mobile telephones, at best a trunk call at great cost. The pace was the key, each generation has a pace. Current and future generations have faster and faster paces, so in order to keep pace with the times there has to be an adjustment somewhere, and that has to be the brain's browser, or processing mechanism. Technology and mental processing advance simultaneously. Each is because of the other. The software is in place in the kids of today, but some kids have software in advance of the technology, and seem hyperactive because they are ready for the next level of pace. Hyperspace reacts naturally and extends its contents and downloads new software, either delivered by its resident entities or by its own consciousness. There are many levels of ADD, some people appear ADD but are not and are wrongly treated. They are just challenged. Then the severely ADD kids who need medication because their chemical neurotransmitters are not enough for today's tasks.

What is important is that if a child appears to suffer from the classic signs of ADD that the child is seen to at the earliest opportunity because if any symptomatic ADD is present and treated the child will not suffer the emotional issues that I have spelled out in this book. The child can be saved and eventually he will come into his or her own.

Symptomatic ADD/ADHD is, I believe, part of the solution and not the problem. It is supplying the minds to tackle the smokescreen and sift through the quagmire of lies perpetrated on us by the media moguls. This takes a very specific type of brain with a very special cosmic processing browser. It opens the way for others to peer inside because the people who open these forbidden doors, do not fear the consequences and they can see the patterns of reality amongst the chaos. This book is not meant to further the cause of any scientific individuals. It is meant to lay all the cards on the table and for you to look at the evidence. My senses tell me that human consciousness has already begun a hyper-leap to the next level and people like Dr Steven Greer have bravely and openly introduced The Disclosure Project, briefly mentioned previously. It is a nonprofit research project working to fully disclose the facts about UFOs, extraterrestrial intelligence, and classified advanced energy and propulsion systems. They have over 400 government, military, and intelligence community witnesses testifying to their direct, personal, first hand experience with UFOs, ETs, ET technology, and the cover-up that keeps this information secret. You can watch the National Press Club Press Conference Video free on Dr Steven Greer's website. With evidence like this, so openly disclosed in front of the press, you have to begin to wonder about the reality I spoke about in the beginning of the book, about how certain things are painted in and how those at the top leading us by the nose hide the real world from you. The subject of Dr Greer is kept out of the mainstream news by the controllers and painters of this world's belief system.

Another hero in the field of psychiatry is the late John Mack. This article was published soon after his death, having been knocked over by a car.

The Times (UK)
23 Oct 2004
John Mack

Psychiatrist who baited orthodoxy by embracing accounts of abduction by extraterrestrials

"JOHN MACK was an unconventional American academic who applied his expertise in psychiatry to the many aspects of civilization he found intriguing or wanting. He won the Pulitzer Prize for his biography of the soldier and author T. E. Lawrence; for many years he taught as a Professor of Psychiatry at Harvard. His research into what he regarded as the spiritual or transformational effects of claimed alien encounters led him to be seen as a proponent of extraterrestrial life. This and his acceptance of alien abduction won him fame and notoriety in equal measure.

John Edward Mack was born into a prosperous New York German-Jewish family in 1929. His parents were academics. His father was a pointedly secular intellectual who, Mack remembered, would read the Bible to John and his sister "not as the word of God, but as a document of great literary importance for our culture and personal education". One uncle was a Holocaust survivor who later became an expert in group process and psychotherapy; another was mentally ill and eventually lobotomised — something Mack described as crucial to his own decision to go into psychiatry.

Mack did an undergraduate degree at Oberlin College, Ohio and went on to Harvard Medical School. He married Sally Stahl in

1959 and spent two years in Japan as an Air Force psychiatrist, then completed advanced training at the Boston Psychoanalytic Society and Institute. He was certified as a child analyst in 1969. He returned to Harvard and became a professor of psychiatry in 1972.

His biography of T.E. Lawrence, 'A Prince of Our Disorder' (1977), for which he received the Pulitzer Prize, was an example of the wide scope of his interests, his dedication to detail and his willingness to draw on every aspect of his training to produce original accessible scholarship. He interviewed a number of people connected with Lawrence, who, before the publication of Mack's book, had been described as a woman-hater, homosexual and even asexual. Mack discovered in an interview with the adventurer's sister-in-law, Janet Laurie that Lawrence had in fact had his heart broken at the age of 21 and never recovered. Lawrence had suddenly and unexpectedly proposed to the beautiful family friend, Miss Laurie, who rejected him for his more dashing older brother.

Mack did not shy away from his own search for self-knowledge, which he realised through less traditional methods as well as through his rigorous academic training. For instance, he practised holotropic breathwork, a technique developed by Stanislav Grof, a pioneer of psychedelic therapy in the 1970s, to bring about a deeper state of consciousness through breathing exercises and evocative music.

This search for self-knowledge led Mack into controversy. He took an active interest in contemporary Middle Eastern politics; he even flew to Lebanon during its civil war to meet Yassir Arafat. He was deeply concerned with the effect of nuclear weapons, and he studied how the fear of a nuclear holocaust affected children. In 1986 he and his family were arrested at the military test site in Nevada, where they were protesting against underground detonations.

Mack believed that there was "an extraordinary planetary crisis because of our inability to understand what native peoples all over the world understand, which is that there is a very delicate web of life, and that web of life is being destroyed by this species".

This view underpinned the ideas for which he will — perhaps wrongly — be most widely remembered. Mack broke from the academic mainstream when he published Abduction: Human Encounters with Aliens (1994), in which he detailed 13 case histories of those who claimed they had been kidnapped and seduced by aliens.

The book was not well received by his peers at Harvard; it precipitated what he called a "15-month ordeal" in which his methods were investigated. Mack felt that if he had simply reported a new "psychiatric syndrome of unknown aetiology" all would have been well. But he was calling for a different interpretation of reality, in effect a broader definition of reality which would accommodate the integration of indigenous peoples' ideas and the consequences of the claimed experience of alien abduction, which he took very seriously.

"I'm not trying to prove this with physical evidence," he said. "These abduction accounts are so congruent among healthy people, from all over the United States — people who are not in touch with each other, who have nothing to gain and everything to lose by telling their stories. The only thing I know that behaves like that is real experience, and I am going to continue to try to deepen my understanding."

Although Mack was open and caring with his patients, his courting of the media was perhaps one reason behind his colleagues' hostility. Abduction and the follow up, Passport to the Cosmos: Human Transformation and Alien Encounters (1999), were works of "popular" science; he appeared on TV and on radio talk shows and gave interviews in the tabloid press. In February 2003 the film Touched appeared — a documentary about his work with those who claimed to have had alien encounters.

Despite the loss of academic credibility, Mack claimed that he was engaged on the most exciting work of his career. He founded the Department of Psychiatry at Cambridge Hospital in Boston and in 1983 he co-founded the Centre of Psychology and Social Change, which was renamed in his honour this year. The centre's declared aim was to apply the new knowledge emerging from exploration of the way in which "perceptions and beliefs about reality shape the human condition to pressing psychological, spiritual and cultural issues."

Mack was an assistant editor of the Journal of the American Psychoanalytic Association and was on the editorial board of the American Journal of Psychoanalysis. He wrote or co-wrote ten books, including the classic psychiatric text Nightmares and Human Conflict, as well as writing 150 scholarly articles.

His interest in Lawrence remained, and it was after speaking *at a T. E. Lawrence Society Symposium in Oxford that he was struck by a car and killed. He and his wife were divorced in 1995. His three sons survive him.*

John Mack, psychiatrist, was born on October 4, 1929. He died on September 27, 2004, aged 74."

Chapter 33

Death of a parent
Or
ADHD celebration of life

The deal had gone quiet and the holidays in Europe were in full force. This leaves Hong Kong rather relaxed. I was wondering how many more personal disclosures I would have to make to the lawyers over this deal. That is a requirement in any acquisition, to dig up any dirty laundry and put it on the table upfront. To be truthful there was very little from any of us. We had really told it as it was. From what I remember, there was nothing that could affect the material outcome of the business once sold. Still, the lawyer's assistant was pressing me and pushing me to get out as much information as possible. There just was not any more than I had disclosed. It was now time to wait till they all came back and my mind drifted back five years ago to the memory of my father, the old Oil Human. He passed away from cancer that had eaten his body from the inside but not before travelling to Australia and South Africa to see his brother and family, perhaps subconsciously realizing it would be for the last time. He did not know that he had cancer; he said he sensed that something was not right and when he came back to London, his bones started to hurt. Accompanied by my mother, the specialist told him he had three months to live. What a shock for my mother. Not so, for my father.

One thing for sure about my family, despite all, is that we were all very close. A sister in London, one in Australia and me in Hong Kong. The cousins were scattered all over the world but always in touch. Death amongst us was never an option, not a possibility. We were all connected. I was only just really getting to know him and getting closer. One thing about me that I can truly say is that I honored my parents, looked after them and always put their well- being right at the top of my priorities. Despite my dad being an Oil human of the nth degree. It was later in life I saw his portals of acceptance slowly open. I guess he figured that after seeing me leave the UK, and actually taking on tasks that would scare the pants of most families, that I was capable. He came to China with me one time and witnessed certain events, like PLA soldiers breaking into our room in case you were cohabiting with a prostitute. He saw me setting up deals with factories and negotiating in tough circumstances. All this must have made him realize that I was not the idiot that he had labeled me. He began to gain pride in me and those last few years were the only years that I had a father who listened and who had interest in me. To some extent, much of what I did was in the hope of him being proud of me. To hear that he had a life threatening condition looming and could have died made me internalize and I realized that I was not ready for this. The poor man lived all his life with certain cardiac events causing him to have irregular heartbeats and these led to dizzy spells and anxiety. It spoiled his life. It might have been this constant pressure that made him so negative.

The doctors found that the problem went by unsolved all his life. He had two nerves leading to his heart instead of one and they were able to burn one out in no time at all. He was cured. He left for a long trip with my mother to enjoy what he had left of his life.

The event that followed was surreal. It changed my views on life and made me rethink my views on death. Various calls were made to me in Hong Kong over the next few weeks. The family all got together in London. He was with his two daughters, grandchildren and of course his wife. At 74, his weight had dropped dramatically and one particular day my sister said we had better come over. They said he was acting strangely and maybe losing his mind. I spoke to him on the telephone and he sounded drunk. He was slurring his words, which happens when a certain nerve is compromised by illness.

I arrived within days and he was so thin but swinging between bouts of elation and bouts of sadness. He said to me that I should go through all his affairs and check that they were all in order. I asked him, "Are you afraid of dying?" He replied that he wasn't, and I asked why?

"Well, I have had enough," he said.

I watched him pull himself upstairs on the handrail but the next time he came down, he needed help back up again. He was on his last legs but all this strange behavior was disturbing. Almost oblivious of the fact that he was dying, he acted as though he had made an appointment. He got into bed, the hospice nurse came around, and it was time to administer morphine patches and have drips at the ready. He really loved the nurses and appreciated all their dedication. I looked at them and wondered what drives a person to give their time to sit with and assist people in their passing. I watched all the interactions and especially the eye contact. They appeared to be angels in that they never looked out of the window, they only looked into his eyes. I thought that is what an angel would do. These women are incredible; they give their lives so others can pass in peace. This is what life is about, reaching this level of losing the concept of 'me'.

Everyone was following the courses of action as though it was a normal day. As the hours went by he started arrangements to leave his earthly container. It started with bouts of being conscious but not talking properly, which deteriorated into grunting sounds but not being able to move, then to not even being able to move his eyes and only if you stood in front of him could he see you and give a reaction, The patches were applied, the morphine pump plugged into him and the journey to heaven had begun. We sat in full realization, as though time had stopped, not knowing what the next course of events would be. A family friend who was a physician said the breathing pattern was a sign of the end in sight within hours. My dad pushed past this barrier, he was breathing badly simply because he had been placed on his back. Once on his side, he was able to breath easier. Now the amazing moments began. People from Leeds where he was born had heard about his impending death. They traveled from all over to come to see him. Some saw him when he was conscious and others did not. The most amazing thing I saw was when a childhood friend, stricken with muscle degeneration and dying himself, arrived. He hobbled out of the car on sticks, crawled up the stairs on his belly, and pulled himself in to the room with tears falling from his eyes. What could we do but stand there and gasp, in disbelief of this desperate picture in front of us.

My mother said to my father, "Paul is here, he has come to see you." It was said out of politeness and respect that Paul had dragged himself up the stairs in tears in order to say goodbye to his old friend. We knew that there would be no reaction. It was too late. In that instant after my dad was told that Paul had come to see him, we worried the fact that there would be no response and a bit of an embarrassment in not satisfying the emotional expectations of a good friend. My father rose up and put both arms around him. The two of them embraced. I watched the tears welling up in the eyes of the family and friends in the room. A sight to be remembered and a sight that made you think about what must be going on in the mind of a person leaving his container behind. Perhaps the transition is a mental process that keeps them busy and maybe the keepers of the light release a little slack on their cosmic umbilical cord, before they rein him in. He lapsed into a coma that was to end in his death the next day. I said my goodbyes several hours before the final moment and left for Hong Kong. My dad was my dad, dead or alive. Since it was the Sabbath, nobody could remove him for burial all day. His grandchildren were in and out of bed with him as though he were alive. The funeral was a strange mix of light heartedness and emotion, the two working hand in hand. It was a day that nobody could understand, and finally after the Sabbath ended the Black Hats of London arrived and carried him out. It was at that point that death became the reality as my sisters ran down the road chasing after the Black Hats screaming for him, crying for him, wanting him back home, dead or alive.

He was buried the next day and life for my mother changed. For me, I had a great sense that I had given back to him and he had given back to me that which we never had in the early days. I am comforted by the fact that I have looked at death through this experience and because of my out-of-body experiences, I am convinced that there is more to death than we can perceive. I feel that because I was able to leave my body on many occasions, then death is the end for the container, but not the soul. I am comforted by the special light that I see when I am out of my container and by the God light emitted from the crafts during the sightings I had in Hong Kong with

Mango. For we are all from light, so is everything we see created, all transcends from light to give this world its mystical purpose. Do not forget that matter is the lowest form of energy. I am tired of seeing programs on TV when they show people who have had spiritual experiences, whether out-of-body, near death experiences or abductions, debunked by science. Debunked by these little men of science, wearing suits and ties, with no ability to use cosmic logical conclusions based on the same evidence acceptable by courts, to determine the possibility that these people have experienced what they say they have. Many scientists are government-funded or high profile in their field and in fairness are afraid of diminishing their credibility. Any drop in credibility means a cut in funding or being pushed into the lunatic fringe. Living in the world of tightly joined squares means that there is no space for them to live between the cracks. Only plants grow in the cracks and joints of the pavements, a cosmic gift to the star seeds.

> *"Humans are beginning to change,to evolve, and are looking for spiritual roots. There is more to God than people get in church"*
> Dr Michael Wolf

"If I become President, I'll make every piece of information this country has about UFO sightings available to the public and scientists. I am convinced that UFOs exist because I have seen one."
PRESIDENT JIMMY CARTER
Presidential campaign 1976

"It was the darndest thing I've ever seen. It was

big, it was very bright, it changed colors, and it was about the size of the moon. A red and green glowing orb radiated as it hurtled across the southwestern Georgia skies. We watched it for ten minutes, but none of us could figure out what it was. One thing's for sure: I'll never make fun of people who say they've seen unidentified flying objects in the sky."

PRESIDENT JIMMY CARTER
Interview following his sighting (with many others) of a UFO at Leary, Georgia
October 1969

Alas, it was made certain that Jimmy Carter would never make every piece of information available to the public!

Chapter 34

How does ET Disclosure make any difference to your life?
Or
Leave me in my comfort zone please

The disclosure of UFOs is a topic that I come across quite often, especially when I am visiting friends. I might add that I do not arrive in such a mode but after people in the room begin to hear about my experiences, the topic of ET seems to arise. Those who have heard me talking about the subject, or witnessed me at a public lecture challenging speakers, are pretty fed up with hearing me discuss the topic, mainly because it bangs on the doors of their comfort zones or stretches their mind on a relaxing night. There are a few people who do want to know more and out of frustration ask this popular question.

"How would the proof of ET make any difference to you personally?"

Whenever I am asked this question in front of American expats, it is very delicate because the answer cuts across their belief system and the core of the problem lies at the heart of the American system. They think they are free but are not. They are fooled to the hilt and the perpetrators are addicted to religion. I normally try to back away or answer as vaguely as possible. The subject has been kept secret by their rogue shadow government that is the military industrial complex and associated covert agencies, for over 60 years. This fact brings the discussion into the arena of politics and then all falls apart.

How do I explain that my facts are certain, that my knowledge capsule steered me to the evidence? What of whistle-blower Dr Michael Wolf, a member of the secret government itself, who told the world his story just before death in a book called *'The Catchers of Heaven'*? He had cloned a human being and accelerated it growth. He was working with ETs at a secret US Military base. National security is on the side of the people but it has its own agenda as well. The people do not understand that national security works for the shadow government; that is why everything to do with UFOs such as the crash at Roswell 1947 undergoes a hasty cover-up. Those in the know are sick of hearing the pitiful stories from the air force that Roswell was not a craft, it was the air force dropping dummies in undergoing certain tests. It was proven that those tests were done in the 1950s. The air force then changed the story and said that the crash was a Mogul balloon used for military intelligence.

So my discussion on how this would change my life is hard to explain to people who are victims of their environment, who watch the carefully censored news on TV. Their belief system and world view is totally painted in and they live in an economy that has geopolitical ambitions, a military industrial complex that needs war in order to sell arms and take control of energy supplies around the world. If all that was smashed by ETs allowing the realities to get through to their minds, all our lives would change dramatically. They have shown that they are here by their numerous displays in the skiesOne example, are the Phoenix lights: U.S. states of Arizona and Nevada, and the Mexican state of Sonora on March 13, 1997.

> "PHOENIX — Former Arizona Gov. Fife Symington trotted out an aide dressed as an alien 10 years ago to spoof the frenzy surrounding mysterious lights in the Phoenix sky. Now he says he saw the lights himself, and believed from the start that they were extraterrestrial."
>
> "I'm a pilot and I know just about every machine that flies," Symington, a former Air Force captain, told the Arizona Daily Star on Thursday.
>
> "It was bigger than anything that I've ever seen. It remains a great mystery. Other people saw it, responsible people. I don't know why people would ridicule it."
>
> "Symington told a major news network the craft he saw March 13, 1997, was "Enormous. It just felt otherworldly. In your gut, you could just tell it was otherworldly."

Despite all the denial and confusion, Dr Lynne Kitei a Phoenix medical practitioner and witness to the sighting, hosts a website, http://www.thephoenixlights.net/index.html dedicated to searching for the truth surrounding this event.

> "Dr. Lynne Kitei, Terri Mansfield and Dr. Rebecca Hardcastle formed Phoenix Lights 3 in 2007 to enhance the public acknowledgment, showcasing and strengthening of Phoenix as a primary gateway for UFO disclosure. The historic Phoenix Lights event was the largest sustained sighting of a UFO in our country in the 20th Century—over a longer period of time and over a larger geographical area than any other UFO sighting in modern times. Phoenix Lights 3 was formed to validate the experiences of the thousands of citizens across Arizona who witnessed the mile-wide craft sighting of March 13, 1997, as well as the tens of thousands of citizens with personal sightings and experiences. Lives changed and perspectives realigned. The possibility of peaceful disclosure is a reality."

"It is the lights and much more."
http://www.phoenixlights3.com/

I was at dinner at my accountant's apartment and around the Sabbath table were some semi-religious members of our community. When I spoke, they listened with concern. The fact that they were concerned was enough for me to slow down and try to use didactics to deliver the message. I delivered the message, cloaked with religious phrases and connotations. In amazement when I did so, their mental digestion worked a treat. Too direct and too truthful, they viewed me as either a wacko or even a devil. I learned so much that night, I understood and cheered the ETs subtle approach of enabling this consciousness to infuse into the minds of people. What amazed me the most was that one of the religiously-slanted guests, a very generous, tough and big hearted lady, had heard me challenge a physicist who came to lecture in Hong Kong at the local synagogue about the way the Good Book matches and supports science. She gave account of my actions that I went up to the man and challenged him head on about ET and that religion and sciences have nothing to do with each other. He threw down his books and told me to talk to the people in Washington. That was a slip of the tongue; what has Washington done to him? Or what has Washington got to do with religion? I accused him of signing the Official Secrets Act and told him he was not being truthful. She heard me talk to him about other matters regarding ETs and admitted seeing this man walk off in a huff and admitted hearing his feeble arguments.

I have done intensive research on the subject of ET and UFOs and their interactions with consciousness. It seemed to be a way to rationalize what happened to me and my face-to-face experiences with Star Visitors. In the same way, abductees tend to gravitate towards the

UFO phenomena for explanations about their experiences. Some meet up with hypnotherapists who are in the UFO loop, or even with authors, researchers and campaigners for the disclosure of this subject. It is no wonder that my research took me deep into ET field of operations, which I might say is littered with hoaxers, government funded scientists and greedy authors out to make a buck. However, there is a residue of dedicated and true activists, many of whom are professionals and have taken great risk to their livelihood and lives to bring the ET question into the public domain.

I would say that even an idiot could answer the question on the difference that disclosure of UFOs would make to me. It has been proven, but paradoxically, people expect the disclosure to come from the very people who lied to them in the first place. Imagine that? They are waiting for their captors to release them. Such is the gap between the current-day human being and the enlightened human being. Then of course, there is the great gap between the human on earth and the Star Visitors, who seek a faster and surer evolution for us ignorant souls. I can only answer the question of what difference would it make to me if ET were proven real, from a very subjective point of view. There is, within most ET related evidence, what they call plausible deniability [13]. This allows for a soft landing for our religious leaders and softens the impact for an uninformed population.

So, to all my good friends, Rabbis, Priests, Teachers and social climbers, here is the difference it would make to all:

- Confirmation that we are not at the top of the food chain. A Challenge to our sense of predominance over the Universe.
- Our true origins; a bioengineered race. A lesson on the real history of mankind and the hidden paleoanthropology. Every museum has 2 doors. Dr Michael Cremo *(www.mcremo.com)*

- Zero Point Energy, free energy from the quantum fabric of space; the propulsion systems for UFOs. Once disclosed it will lead to the defeat of the trans global petroleum villains who have kept this science well hidden (as testified in 2001 by disclosure project witnesses). A lesson in how to take the 80 percent of the world population out of the poverty trap within thirty years and bring them into the economy. This will lead to a green economic revolution.
- Free energy to desalinate seawater. A lesson in bioengineering, planting forests in the desert and making more areas of earth habitable once again.
- An abundance of clean drinking water for all. A lesson in averting wars over water due to free energy desalinating the seawater.
- Monopolies broken on back engineered ET technology. A lesson in the importance of transparency in government.
- New technology taken from the old black budget projects. A lesson in medicine, regeneration of limbs and organs. A lesson in new, sophisticated healthcare for all.
- Anti gravity. Buildings erected above the Earth's surface, fully powered by non-polluting, sustainable resources. A lesson in real environmental improvements.
- Clean air and healthier kids. A lesson in caring for the planet.
- Movement towards peace, geopolitics replaced with exopolitics, politics which include the citizens and institution and their diplomatic interactions with all star visitor nations.
- Abolition of nuclear weapons on land and in space. A lesson in peace and galactic cooperation.
- Education in new technologies (e.g. nanotechnology, thought activation, teleportation etc) leading to a world of abundance.

> *Concerning the U.S. government's slow pace of disclosure about UFO reality, Dr Wolf commented, "The government is doing a balancing act, because if Free [Zero-Point] Energy and all the ET technology come out all at once, it'd hurt the stockholders [in obsolescent industries]. The multinational corporations don't want to lose their power.*

I might just add that everything I have said will not only make the difference to me but will make the difference to you all. Our man-made religions have not succeeded in anything past death and destruction, breeding fear and superstition. The words *"You will be judged"* as quoted in religions should be cast away for good and the religious leaders educated into modern times. Many are trying as a last resort to link religion with science as a last resort to hitch a ride on the back of science in case their whole world disappears down the plughole due to disclosure. The religious are secretly praying that the Ganesh particle or any other new quantum particle found might be god himself. If they could succeed in such an endeavor, we would be stuck with them for another few thousand years. Religious traditions will remain since many basic principles are universal. The nature of life will be spiritual. Whether Christian, Catholic, Muslim or Jewish, a helping hand is always welcome and the old traditions enjoyable within the family unit and friends. The message is clear, we all have to learn by ourselves and follow the clues of our experiences and gut feelings. We must open our senses to the language of the universe (remember the forest has its own language, shapes and eco system, so does the universe). Cast out anyone who preaches to you religious stories of fire and brimstone, judgments and so on. We are all highly developed spiritual beings ready to burst forwards and the last thing you need is a ball and chain of antiquated fairy tales to hold you back.

Give a helping hand to the next person and he will do the same for you. If he does not, give repeatedly and again. The spiritual laws of the universe are important, a universe run by cause and effect and it is older than we all are.

The extraterrestrials traverse the galaxy by manipulating space and time to pull their destination towards them. "Time is reduced to zero, and acceleration is increased to infinity. Dr Michael Wolf

Chapter 35

Why don't the Star Visitors show themselves?

The question I am asked most frequently is, "If ETs exist, why don't they just reveal themselves to us? In the previous chapter, I stated the benefits we could gain from ETs. In this chapter, I will explain why I believe they have not revealed themselves, and the possible negative repercussions that could result from doing so. There are people in high places, in positions of responsibility. You can recall some of the greatest tyrants in the world holding out despite their civilians being bombed. There are those who systematically allow drugs to pass through their borders, drugs that kill and destroy lives. There are those who care not of the Forests and those who care not of the destruction of the atmosphere from pollution. Worst of all there are those who will go out in the name of economics and kill others to take their natural resources. The list grows longer and longer and the conclusion has to be that our leaders are corrupted by power and money. They have lost their footing in the real world and their actions have taken a toll on the citizens of earth. The painted-in bits are there to stop you seeing this truth whilst those tyrants send your kids to war.

By now, we should have been using free energy, breathing cleaner air. Transport would have been on a completely new level. We would have had many people pulled out of the poverty trap and higher standards of living would allow a natural process to occur where less people are born each year, reducing overpopulation and talking the strain off the diminishing resources of the planet. However, the rogue shadow governments hide this technology from us, as they stand to gain so much more from exploiting our planet. President Eisenhower was reported to have had a meeting with Extra Terrestrials in 1954 at Edwards Air force base [14]. I give you a quote from President Eisenhower's historic farewell address to the nation in Jan 1961.

"In the counsels of Government, we must guard against the acquisition of unwarranted influence, whether sought or unsought, by the Military Industrial Complex. The potential for the disastrous rise of misplaced power exists, and will persist. We must never let the weight of this combination endanger our liberties or democratic processes. We should take nothing for granted. Only an alert and knowledgeable citizenry can compel the proper meshing of the huge industrial and military machinery of defense with our peaceful methods and goals so that security and liberty may prosper together."

- President Eisenhower - January 1961

The president was concerned that the Military industrial complex would hijack humanity, which it certainly did. Without fear of turning this very honest book into a non mainstream media carnival, I have to say that the underlying situation here is that the earth human has not been allowed to evolve and consequently man's belief system has been so polluted that very few can really see the light. Another factor is that we are controlled by fear. You hear it and see it every day on the TV. Hence the ADHD wired brain, which can in most cases see through the fog, speaks out fear free, to assist in leading us all to the way out. Please keep an open mind to this point. You have nothing to lose; we have been at war over geopolitics and are now in a new war over man god religious doctrine by the hijacking of religion. You have nothing to lose and all to gain by understanding this chapter. If you remain viscous like oil, in your thinking, then you can expect more of the same dreadful news for the rest of your lives. If you start to think, flow free like water and see through the fog, we have the best chance to evolve with greater speed and most important, all together.

Start to remove the painted pictures from the template of your mind and your old belief systems will reboot. Start to learn and let your mind evolve from what you find out, not from what you are told, nor from what society expects you to say and believe. Do not have your nose pulled. If the Brussels sprouts are soggy, throw them away, if the wine tastes like vinegar, send the bottle back.

As promised, here are some of the problems I believe would occur if ETs revealed themselves.

1. The stock market would crash, economic mayhem would ensue and oil shares would tumble. A person quite high up in the military was heard to state: *"If you ever find out that they are going to release the UFO secret tomorrow, be sure you sell everything you have today, because tomorrow everything will be worth nothing."*
2. Possible false flag operations would occur. Black-operative ARV's, *(alien reproduction vehicles)* military saucers with retro-engineered technology from captured spacecrafts,

would bomb civilian landmarks and blame the ETs in order to turn the people against them.
3. Many religious leaders would have to account for the nonsense that they taught. Religion as we know it would implode as people would no longer live in fear of judgment by a god with a small "g". The religious institutions would lose their grip.
4. Science would have to be rewritten. The 1961 Brooking Institute study looked at this situation. "*It has been speculated that of all groups, scientists and engineers might be the most devastated by the discovery of relatively superior creatures, since these professions are most clearly associated with the mastery of nature, rather than with the understanding and expression of man.*"
5. The people would be emotionally hurt when they realize that the very people they voted for and believed in have fooled them or been fooled themselves. A hard one to swallow.
6. In a few cases, the physical appearance of the Star visitors might disturb some people. However, many are extremely humanoid and look like us.
7. Abductions and upgrades: It would prompt people to ask the President, who is constitutionally responsible for the protection of the American people? It is estimated that seven million people report having been abducted by the extraterrestrials. Based on current evidence it appears that not only does the President not know how to stop it, he does not even know why the aliens are doing it
8. Our paleocontact has shown how humans have worshipped the ETs as gods. This time round, the public

> needs a period of acclimation and a gentle detachment from the worldview into the new reality.

I think I need not go deeper into this, nor do I want to, but there is enough brief explanation for you. If so, then the remedy is that we need to wake up to the circles in the fields and UFOs flying in the sky and press our governments for more information. Just be aware of this new flow of cosmic consciousness, which is now coming our way. People are rejecting war, people accusing governments of control by fear, people fighting global warming, green action groups arriving faster than we can write their names down. We can see that there is this second stage of help coming our way, (*the first was the internet*) to prevent those rogues from painting further false pictures into our reality to keep us blind to the truth, whilst a handful benefit from financial rewards.

People ask so many times if the dimensional folk are good or bad? With their technology and level of evolution, they could have taken us out long ago, but did not. In a very compelling exopolitical article I read recently it was pointed out that we might be the only type of civilization in our Galaxy that eat whilst others starve, that are capable of destroying themselves and their planet and who are heading that way. How embarrassing that we continue as if nothing is going on. We must get the truth out. It is then easier to put in the infrastructure, to limit the fall out whilst we take the next giant step forward. Disclosure is a process, which will take at least 10 years to peel back the layers of our painted-in realities. We have to act responsibly and prepare the world for the changes without disrupting it and throwing people into chaos. Religious institutions should be transformed as opposed to disintegration. Our academics must be allowed to take time to understand the realities of the new sciences, which will be made available. Our economies will be able to ride the tide of new technologies and progress will create greater employment' we will move from a society based on winners and losers.

A new infrastructure was born out of necessity; Exopolitics has been created; the study of key individuals, political institutions and processes associated with extraterrestrial life. Exopolitical representatives from many countries have set up websites and centers for disseminating news which bypasses the mainstream media. It is a growing force, which has already made its mark. Activist Stephen Basset was instrumental in submitting exopolitical questions on TV to Presidential candidates during the US elections. One of the candidates replied that he had seen a UFO over the home of actress Shirley Maclaine. His name is Dennis Kucinich [15].

The Exopolitics Institute was founded by Dr Michael Salla PhD and assisted by Angelika Whitecliff in 2005. He is author of *Exopolitics: Political Implications of the Extraterrestrial Presence* (Dandelion Books, 2004), *Exposing U.S. Government Policies on Extraterrestrial Life* (Exopolitics Institute 2009) and founder of the popular website: Exopolitics.Org. He has held full time academic appointments at the Australian National University, and American University, Washington DC. He has a PhD in Government from the University of Queensland and an MA in Philosophy from the University of Melbourne, Australia. During his professional academic career, he was best known for organizing a series of citizen diplomacy initiatives for the East Timor conflict that received large financial grants from the United States Institute of Peace and the Ford Foundation. The institute takes a scholarly approach to the subject of Exopolitics and has created certification courses, thus spreading the light and putting qualified people into place to assist in preparing mankind for disclosure and a post disclosure world of transparency in government.

Angelika Sareighn Whitecliffis a multi-disciplinary researcher involved in the study of consciousness, multidimensional communications and humanity's extraterrestrial origin. She has been a conscious clairvoyant and telepath since childhood, and has been actively communicating with beings of different vibrational frequencies her entire life. Angelika has also had several physical interactions with benevolent, human extraterrestrials that are here to assist humanity in a planet wide spiritual awakening. Angelika helped co-found the Exopolitics Institute with its legal launch in April 7, 2005 as a non-profit corporation in the State of Hawaii

Paola Harris, MEd. is the International Director of the Institute. She is an Italo-American photojournalist and investigative reporter in the field of extraterrestrial related phenomena research. She has studied extraterrestrial related phenomena since 1979 and is on personal terms with many of the leading researchers in the field. From 1980-1986 she assisted Dr. J. Allen Hynek with his UFO investigations and has interviewed many top military witnesses concerning their involvement in the government truth embargo. In 1997, Ms. Harris met and interviewed Col. Philip Corso in Roswell, New Mexico and became a personal friend and confidante. She was instrumental in having his book *The Day After Roswell*, for which she wrote the preface, translated into Italian. She returned to Roswell in the summer of 2003 for the American debut of her book, *Connecting the Dots…making sense of the UFO Phenomena* (Granite Press). Her recent book *"All the Above"* is an exopolitical masterpiece. Paola has consulted with many researchers about the best avenues for planetary disclosure with emphasis on the "big picture" and stressing the historical connection. She is a close friend of Monsignor Padre Corrado Balducci and assisted in filming the Italian witnesses, including the Monsignor, for the Disclosure Project for the May 9, 2001 press conference. She was instrumental in bringing to Italy Robert Dean, Dr. Steven Greer, Linda Moulton Howe, Dr. Richard Boylan, Russell Targ, Travis Walton, Derrell Sims, Helmut Lamner, Michael Lindemann, Nick Pope, Bill Hamilton, Carlos Diaz and Dr. John Mack. Her new non-profit association, Starworks Italia, will continue to bring speakers to Italy and promote disclosure and exopolitical dialogue worldwide. She has been a speaker on many radio shows and conferences in Italy, San Marino, Belgium and Germany, and has appeared many times on Italian TV. She has written for Nexus, UFO Magazine, Notizario UFO and Dossier Alieni, among others publications. Paola lives in Rome and has a Masters degree in Education. Her principal website is: www.paolaharris.com

Rebecca Hardcastle, PhD, is a global expert and leader in Exoconsciousness: the extraterrestrial origins, dimensions and abilities of human consciousness. Her investigations include determining the biological, historical and multidimensional relationship between humans and extraterrestrials. Though once thought beyond human capability, her research normalizes paranormal abilities as essential for a 21st Century space-faring species. Exoconsciousness posits practical applications of advanced consciousness, within and beyond the brain.

> *"Humans possess an extraterrestrial consciousness, or exoconciousness, integral to our bodies and our minds. We possess a cosmic consciousness which links us directly to what the ancients called the 'star visitors' and we term 'extraterrestrials'. Human consciousness is directly linked to the cosmos and its inhabitants."*

An Extraterrestrial experiencer since early childhood, her recent book, *Exoconsciousness: Your 21st Century Mind* details her contact through story, metaphysics, quantum science and ancient knowledge. Committed to fostering the groundbreaking Ufology work of Harvard's John Mack, she applies contemporary scientific traumatology techniques to reframe and rewire trauma scars that often skew the perception of extraterrestrial contact.

Hardcastle is on the faculty of International Metaphysical University http://intermetu.com, where she teaches Exoconsciousness as well as Coaching and Hypnotherapy Protocols for Extraterrestrial Contact. She maintains a private practice in Exoconsciousness Coaching and hypnotherapy. For more information see: www.exoconsciousness.com and www.rebeccahardcastle.com

Hardcastle advocates for psychiatric and cultural acceptance of paranormal experience as normal, including extraterrestrial contact. Her work encompasses research and validation of psychic intelligence, experience and abilities.

Dedicated to empowering the planet's citizenry to create an Extraterrestrial Reality through Exoconsciousness, she is affiliated with Quantrek http://www.quantrek.org a non-profit founded by Apollo 14 astronaut, Edgar Mitchell, that combines science and spirituality in quantum physics and cosmology for public education, scientific research and development of practical applications of new forms of energy. Within Quantrek, she and Terri Mansfield, a recognized International peace diplomat, are Co-Directors of Peace Exoconsciousness. Hardcastle is also a Partner with Fundraising in the Public Interesta fundraising firm that specializes in endowments for social change, including zero-point energy applications promoting planetary sustainability. July 4, 2008, she co-founded

ET VOTE NOW, www.etvotenow.org a planetary and national initiative to establish a Department of Extraterrestrial Alliances. This governmental department would be responsible for open diplomatic relations with extraterrestrials and public dissemination of UFO/ET information. Supporting the necessary unification of Exopolitics and Exoconsciousness, she is a long-standing member of the Research and Education Advisory Board of Exopolitics Institute.

In 2005, she taught Extraterrestrial Reality at Scottsdale Community College, one of the first Ufology courses in the nation. Her professional background included the directorship of an ecumenical chaplain program at Wright State University in Dayton, Ohio. An ordained Elder in the United Methodist Church, Hardcastle served on national boards and agencies for the denomination. She has a doctorate in Parapsychic Science from American Institute of Holistic Theology and a Masters in Divinity from Boston University School of Theology. Hardcastle is committed to peacefully transitioning mainstream science, religion, technology, medicine, government, business and education into an emerging Extraterrestrial Reality formed by Ufology, Exopolitics and Exoconsciousness.

Such are the changes filling our reality and so dedicated are the cosmic forces above; that they are helping us to help ourselves in dissolving the impediments of this world. Alfred Webre, the inventor of the term "Exopolitics" can be heard weekly on his Internet radio program (www.exopolitics.com) along with George Noory on Coast to Coast radio (www.coasttocoastam.com). The Kevin Smith show invites the public to challenge his guests, many of whom are operatives within the theatre of Exopolitics.

Stephen Basset, founder of the Paradigm research group (www.paradigmresearchgroup.org) lobbies members of Congress and his website hosts the largest archive of exopolitical video clips, newspaper articles and his well known paradigm clock, which ticks away alerting the world to the time when governments will have formally acknowledged the extra terrestrial presence.

The earth is changing and so are its frequencies. We must reach out and touch them, connect and realize that we are climbing the ladder of evolution. DNA is spontaneously erupting and our interdimensional manipulators are applauding us, pressing us to go forth into the new reality, together as one….as I did when Peter, Ricky and I worked together to escape from the quicksand of the swamp in Durban North.

Chapter 36

The Finale

The day before I was due to leave for a Washington conference, hosted every year by Exopolitics activist, Stephen Basset, I was on the balcony at 8.00pm on 12th September 2007. We lived on the 13th floor and the apartment's balcony faces the sea to the South-West. We had guests, an accountant friend and his wife. My youngest son, my daughter and my wife were also present. My son had a laser pointer which we were flicking on and off into the clear night sky. I had mentioned to my son on many occasions that a CE5 (*close encounter by calling in a craft*) protocol exists, one of the tools to attract crafts being a laser beam, along with other pulsing implements. It brought a smirk to people's faces, yet the glow in my son's eyes, sparks of interest, allowed me to carry on talking about it despite the obvious background sniggering. The accountant, whom I went to school with, had been in Hong Kong for about six months and to him UFOs had to be seen to be believed. He was with one of the top five firms in the world.

They were all fascinated by what we were doing on the balcony. Suddenly my son and I looked up to where we had been flashing the beam and saw appear out of nowhere directly above us a huge V shaped craft with lights underneath its wings. It flew from the South to the North, silently and slowly. I had seen this craft or similar before in 2000 over Hong Kong when I reported it to MUFON. (Mutual UFO Network)

I shouted for everyone to look up at the UFO. I was filled with emotion because at last my wife and kids would be able to witness what I had seen and spoken about in the past. Our visitors were stunned to the extent that questions were being asked all night with regular visits back to the balcony with the accountant flashing the laser beam, bringing a smile to my face. This meant everything to me.

My son has been so excited since then and my wife is somewhat bewildered. Our friends were stunned to say the least; it was a new awakening for them. On my part, I am still so happy that at last my family saw what I saw in 2000. This craft was over a kilometer wide. It was at very high altitude but very clear to look at. My size estimation is based on my last sighting when it was at 800ft altitude calibrated against a well-known Hong Kong building, which had a beam of light on the top as part of the design. I had worked out its height approximately. This craft resembled the witness drawings of the Phoenix lights as opposed to the film clips because it had solid wings with lights. The solidity of the wings seemed to be invisible in the last few seconds and only the lights were clearly visible. It literally vanished in front of our eyes after about 7 seconds. I do not wish to sound arrogant but I am more than convinced that this appearance of our Star Visitors was there for a reason concerning my state of mind. It was there to bring closure to me and my family of the extraordinary events in writing this book and for the journey I had written about. I was absolved of being 'mad'. It is my duty to let you all know what I was allowed to see during my sojourn. I emphasize that I was allowed to see this world as it overlapped the dimensions above, using the software given to me by the Star Visitors. There is a difference, because I cannot be accused of being a preacher, or compared to a person who wants to start a cult. *I tell it as it is.*

'Catch Me If You Can', a film, a true story of a man called Frank Abagnale. Obviously ADD beyond all doubt, Frank was a conman who masqueraded as an airline pilot and many other roles in order to defraud the airline by forging cheques. His integrity put aside for a moment, it was quite amazing how he was able to get in between the cracks of society's systems, so much so that in the end, the FBI released him from jail on condition that he worked for them, helping them to crack down on this type of crime.

Somewhere in the film, they spoke of a story of two mice that fell into a bowl of cream. One (Oil) gave up and drowned, the other (Water) struggled so hard for so long and never gave up, until the cream hardened and turned into butter. The mouse simply crawled out of the bowl and survived.

A week later, the deal was signed.

> *"Everything that we see is a shadow cast by that which we do not see." Martin Luther King*

On the 4th June 2009 the writer graduated from the Exopolitics Institute Certification Program and in 2010 was invited to join its Board of Directors.

Bibliography

[1] Sleep Paralysis: *abduction experiences can be differentiated from traumatic reactions to sleep paralysis because a portion of abduction takes place during the day and these reports show clear similarities to reports whch occur at night. Experiencers report similar details and procedures that go unreported in the media that are present across cultures and young children. Sleep paralysis cannot account for these common details. Experiencers show that anxiety and nightmares tend to resolve with the conscious processing of abduction material which would seem unlikely if the traumatic experience was not directly linked to the material. Furthermore Mack et all explain that sleep paralysis and hypnogogic hallucinations of such durations tend to be symptoms of narcolepsy – a neural disorder characterized by an overwhelming desire to sleep at any time. Individuals with narcolepsy also suffer from cataplexy (Carlson 1994) a sudden los of voluntary muscle tonus with full conciousness, often during emotional events; McLeod, Corbisier and Mack deny such symptoms. Those experiencers who have undergone electroencephalograph tests (EEG) in an attempt to find neurological cause for their experiences report no significant findings. Attempt to link abduction experiences to normal neurology such as sleep paralysis has not been successful."* A **More Parsimonious Explanation for UFO Abduction;** download at http://www.michaelsheiser.com/UFORcligions/A%20More%20Parsimonious%20Explanation%20for%20UFO%20Abduction.pdf

[2] NICAP Website at: http://www.nicap.org/ncp/ncp-home.htm

[3] Mind Control and Brainwashing website at: http://www.phinnweb.org/neuro/brainwash/

[4] Free E Book: *The Diamond Invention* by Edward J Epstein. Website at: http://www.edwardjayepstein.com/diamond/prologue.htm

[5] Near Death Experiences; website at: http://www.near-death.com/

[6] T&G; tongued and grooved wooden wall cladding, 9mm x 95mm boards, cut to length and shrink-wrapped. Made from Pine and Hardwoods.

[7] Ritalin is used to treat ADD and ADHD. See website at: http://pediatrics.about.com/od/adhdmedications/p/05_ritalin.htm

[8] Crystal Children: Website at http://www.mastersinstitute.org/indigo.html

[9] Article on Secret Societies, website at http://www.indiadaily.com/editorial/06-19-04.asp

[10] Media truth Embargo website at: http://www.exopolitics.org.uk/the-truth-embargo-on-extra%11terrestrial-intelligence/

[11] Black Budget 1.7 Trillion Dollars. Website at http://www.exopolitics.org/Report-Black-Budget.htm

[12] Project Camelot interview Command Sergeant Bob Dean (Retired). Websites at http://www.youtube.com/watch?v=VI9fS8Y-fww and http://www.youtube.com/watch?v=X5vjv3e9xAo&feature=related

[13] Plausible deniability website at: Plausible deniability http://www.tjresearch.info/denial.htm

[14] Eisenhower met ETS in 1954. Website at: http://www.exopolitics.org/Study-Paper-8.htm

[15] Dennis Kucinich UFO video at: http://www.youtube.com/watch?v=gSRWRbuMqyc

About the Author

Neil Gould is a multi-faced individual who combines a variety of business practices with ET contact/disclosure advocacy. His is a landmark book, presenting for the first time the thesis that in some cases [not all cases] the symptoms of what is known as ADHD, rather than being an affliction are in fact the result of an advanced form of consciousness that comes with childhood extra terrestrial contact. Born in South Africa in 1954 he and his family emigrated to the United Kingdom in 1974 before finally residing in China and Hong Kong in 1995. An ADHD challenged author wired into a multidimensional reality, Neil has endured contact experiences with off world beings. Previously judged as a man who lived in a world of fantasy by his peers and family, it was not long before these views were dispelled; a craft of gigantic proportion appeared close up in front of him, his family and friends in Hong Kong, but not before morphing from a bat winged shape into a circular donut shape which then became transparent. Frustrated by the experiences, Neil found his peace within the Exopolitics Institute, founded by Dr Michael Salla PhD assisted by Angelika Whitecliff in 2005. Neil graduated from the Institutes Certification Program in 2009. In 2010 Dr Salla invited him to join the Exopolitics Institute's Board of Directors. Neil's activities include lecturing on exopolitics, co-hosting a Hong Kong Exopolitical Radio program, producing Exopolitical films on

YouTube and developing alternative and cleaner energy technologies with his production facilities in China.